How to Write and Publish a Scientific Paper:
The Step-by-Step Guide

How to Write and Publish a Scientific Paper:

The Step-by-Step Guide

Dr. Luz Claudio

Write Science Now Publishing Co.
San Juan, PR
New York, NY

Printed in the United States of America

First Printing, 2014

ISBN 978-0-9960110-1-3

107 University Place
New York, NY 10003

Dedicated to my students.
I have learned so much from all of you.

And with love, to my husband and daughter
for everything.

Table of Contents

About the Author

Luz Claudio grew up in the interior countryside of Puerto Rico. The one-way dirt road up the mountain to her childhood home was dotted with the homes of her aunts and uncles, culminating at the top with her grandparents' home and small farm.

Luz's first job was to help her grandmother concoct medicines from plants and herbs from her garden. Thinking that one small orchid-type flower could lower blood sugar, she and her uncle submitted a "research" paper to *Scientific American*. Although swiftly rejected for "lack of experimental evidence," Luz understood at 11 years old that science and writing went hand-in-hand.

Although Luz grew up speaking Spanish, she read most of her science textbooks in English. At 22, she moved to New York City after being accepted on a scholarship to the doctoral program at the Albert Einstein College of Medicine. Under the generous mentoring of Dr. Celia Brosnan, Luz completed her PhD in neuropathology. Before graduating, she had already published 11 papers and two book chapters in some of the most highly rated journals in neurobiology and pathology.

After graduation, Luz was awarded a prestigious Environmental Science and Engineering Fellowship from the American Association for the Advancement of Science. During that time, she worked at the US Environmental Protection Agency to conduct an assessment of the regulatory process for neurotoxic chemicals. This work resulted in two peer-reviewed research papers that were awarded the Robert C. Barnard Environmental Science Award.

In 1991, Dr. Claudio joined the faculty of Mount Sinai School of Medicine, ranked among the top 20 medical schools in the nation. Luz has climbed up the academic ladder at Mount Sinai and is now serving as a tenured professor in the Department of Preventive Medicine and Chief of the Division of International Health.

She serves in numerous national and international committees and is a well-recognized expert in environmental health research. She has published over 80 papers in peer-reviewed journal articles and book chapters and currently sits on the editorial board for two medical journals.

Luz is especially well regarded as a mentor and educator. She directs several training programs, including programs targeting disadvantaged or minority students. Luz has directly mentored 44 graduate students, 57 US and international postdoctoral fellows (many from non-English speaking countries) and overseen the instruction of 110 students on global health research placements.

Throughout her career, Dr. Claudio has developed methods for teaching students to write and publish research papers. She has taught these methods to undergraduate and graduate students, postdoctoral fellows, junior faculty and community-based leaders. Her motto, WRITING SCIENCE RIGHT, is the basis for this book.

Author's Preface

The purpose of this guide is to get you writing and publishing your research papers right NOW!

There will be no long-winded explanations, no blah-blah-blah about literary styles, no on-and-on about punctuation and grammar rules that you likely know already.

This book is geared towards researchers and academics who are ready to publish their work. This book and the accompanying course are perfect for you if:

- You have a fairly good mastery of your language including grammar,
- You have read research papers in your field,
- Your research mentor doesn't have time to teach you the specifics on how to write a research paper,
- You have written reports for your college classes,
- You are in academia as either a student, research assistant, postdoctoral fellow or junior faculty, and you understand that the key to success is to publish your research.

In this book, you will learn:

- How to find out whether your data is ready for publication,
- How to get you and your materials organized,
- How to start and continue writing,
- How to break down the project into doable tasks,
- How to prioritize your writing and find the time to do it,
- How to work with research mentors and collaborators to complete a paper,
- How to choose a journal for your manuscript,
- How to receive and respond to critiques,
- How to repurpose existing material,
- How to promote your research results so that they benefit you and the world.

I will take you step-by-step through the process of writing your research. I will tell you what to do and when to do it to get the most done in the least amount of time. If you follow these steps, you will be able to write and submit your research paper. Anyone who plans to thrive as a researcher will benefit from reading this book, doing the carefully planned exercises and/or taking my course Write Science Now.

If you already have publishable data, you will be able to put together your paper as you go through each step. If you are writing a paper while following along with this book, you should read one chapter of this book, and then follow all the instructions and steps for that chapter before moving onto the next. This book is not a novel; it is a how-to book. Use it. Follow the steps. Write as you read.

Keep this book next to your computer. If you are using the printed format of this book, make use of the margins and other white spaces provided to write notes. **You can also download fillable forms at** www.drluzclaudio.com. This book is designed to get down and dirty with you in the trenches of peer-review publication. Coffee stains and highlighter marks are expected.

I have created a companion online course, *Write Science Now*, found at: www.WriteScienceNow.com. In this course, you will find mentoring, direct instruction, motivation and a community of smart academics who are in the same boat as you are. There is a lot of support in our community forums. Use this book on its own or as a workbook companion to the online course. Either way, you win!

Research publication is an honor and a challenge with many rewards and many frustrations. The methods presented here are designed to increase your opportunities for reward while minimizing the anxiety and frustration that you may experience along the way.

These methods were developed for investigators just like you—students, new researchers and community leaders who are conducting excellent scientific work, and have yet to experience the thrill of being a published author or are looking to improve their writing productivity.

I wish you much success as a published scientist!

− Dr. Luz Claudio

Chapter 1: Publish or Perish, so Write Your Science Research Paper Now

"Research serves to make building stones out of stumbling blocks."

– **Arthur D. Little**, chemist credited with the discovery of acetate.

Search for a generic image of a scientist on the web. Do it now. Just type "scientist" into Google Images. What do you see?

You will likely see row after row of pictures of people in white coats. What are they doing? Pipetting. Mixing test tubes with colorful liquids in a lab. Looking into a microscope…

This is the image that I had of what it would be like to be a scientist. Serious-looking people, mostly men, doing sciencey things. At least now, you will find that many of these stock photos of the prototypical scientist include women. That's improvement! But still. Is it a realistic view of what scientists do every day?

In college, I filled out an aptitude questionnaire to help me through my career choices. It said that you need to be "good with your hands" and "good at math" for a career in science. So I focused on taking advanced calculus and spending extra time doing internships. I spent little time taking courses in literature, writing or the humanities above from what was required to graduate.

Little did I know that as I climbed up the academic ladder, I would end up increasingly needing those writing skills. As I progressed from postdoctoral training, faculty appointments and academic promotions, I started to spend less and less time in the lab doing the sciencey things that I thought all scientists do.

Slowly but surely, I started using my skilled hands and math proficiency that are necessary for experiments less often. Instead, I noticed a shift in the skills that I really needed to succeed in academia—I needed to write. Soon, it felt as if writing grant proposals and research papers was all that I was doing.

Being a scientist, I had to measure this feeling of shifting towards more scientific writing in my working life. When I was an assistant professor, I tracked every minute of my working time in a log for a whole month. I discovered that, even at that early stage in my career, I was spending

For the companion online course, *Write Science Now*, go to www.WriteScienceNow.com.

67% of my time writing. Whether it was research papers or grant proposals, the bulk of my time was being spent in front of my computer putting science into words. It became clear to me that I needed to focus on these writing skills in order to succeed in research. Therefore, learning to write effectively became the focus of my career development strategy.

I bet this is not unusual. If you are an experimental or laboratory scientist, you likely began your career by getting your hands dirty in the lab, or working in the field collecting data from your experiments and observations. Maybe this is still where you are today. But before you know it, conducting experiments and getting the primary data will be delegated to the students and trainees working with you, leaving you with the main task of getting the word out about your discoveries and keeping your team funded.

So you'd better prepare yourself for this shift in the skills that are required for being a successful scientist. And you'd better make the process of writing as efficient as possible so that you can succeed.

How do researchers become writers?

Here you may ask, what do I write about if I don't have time to do the research? Good question.

Well, the process of shifting from spending most of your time doing the experiments and collecting data to spending most of your time writing happens gradually. It is a process that happens as you grow in your profession and start climbing the academic ladder.

As a PhD student, you spend your days attending classes and conducting experiments in the lab or in the field—collecting data. Mostly, you learn the techniques from the lab technicians, senior students and postdocs in the lab who work under the supervision of the principal investigator. What is the principal investigator doing most days? Lecturing at courses or conferences, attending meetings, troubleshooting lab issues and locked up in their office, writing.

To give you an idea of what your mentor may be doing locked up in their office all day, here's a clue: The success rate for RO1s (funding mechanism for health-related research supported by the National Institutes of Health) is about 15%. Writing just one of these proposals can take one or two months of intense work.

Let's say that an investigator has a better than average success rate of 20%. It is not uncommon for a researcher to send five proposals for every one that gets funded. At one to two months of writing per proposal, it doesn't take a math genius to conclude that this means a lot of time will be dedicated to writing grant proposals.

Add to that the amount of time that the principal investigator spends writing research papers, and you have someone who has effectively become a writer.

It happens gradually to most of us. It starts when you write your dissertation and coauthor a few papers, but the pressure to write really kicks in during your second or third year as a postdoc when you find yourself in the unending world of searching for grant funding to become an independent researcher.

At that point, you may also discover that your chances of getting funding are increased tremendously if you have peer-reviewed research papers. The papers will give you a better standing and credibility in the field and will help to distinguish you as an independent scientist—someone apart from your previous mentors. Yet, even though writing papers will be increasingly crucial to your success, you will receive very little (if any) training specifically on how to write and publish research papers. This is a skill that you are expected to pick up along the way, as if through osmosis, or from your mentor, when she/he finds the time.

And such is the life of a research scientist. Still, science is an exciting and vibrant profession. It is fun to think of new ideas for research projects, to design a study that will answer a research question, to advance the level of knowledge a bit further, to share that knowledge with others and to always explore new areas that were previously unknown. I don't lament about the days of pipetting media into petri dishes. For me, communicating the discoveries of my team by writing papers and grant proposals is just as important and satisfying. It is what we do.

What is academic research, then?!

Well, according to the National Science Foundation: "Research is defined as systematic study directed toward fuller scientific knowledge or understanding of the subject studied".

In that sense, to me, academic research is the search for knowledge using the scientific method. One thing that this definition does not say until much later is that most of this "knowledge" lives in peer-reviewed research papers. Research papers are the way that scientists communicate with each other, spread the word about their discoveries and make it possible for scientific knowledge to expand.

What is a peer-reviewed research paper?

 A peer-reviewed research paper (also known as a refereed or scholarly publication) is an article that documents a research study and which has been subjected to the scrutiny of other experts in the field. Therefore, writing a research paper is similar to most non-fiction writing; it should be straightforward, to-the-point, organized and clear. A research paper is not a mystery novel! Scientific research writing aims to be clear and precise, leaving little to the imagination. But because scientific writing deals with complex topics, creating a straightforward, clear paper can be a challenge.

In science writing, your mission is to present your research with the utmost clarity, in a way that allows other scientists to replicate your methods and results. Your research paper should not read as a whodunit, nor should it leave the reader struggling to decipher what you mean or what will happen next.

Instead, your paper's structure should flow like that of a good cookbook; your paper should include all of the details the reader needs in order to understand the *WHO*, *WHY*, the *HOW*, the *WHAT* and the *SO WHAT* of your research, and come away understanding how your results fit into the broader scientific literature.

> *Research publication is vital for scientific advancement.*
> *Peer review is the hallmark of scientific publication.*

The importance of peer-reviewed research publications to your academic career

Why is it so important to publish research papers? The achievement of research publication is so crucial in the professional life of a scientist (especially in academia), that it is often described using the phrase "publish or perish." The quality and quantity of a scientist's published papers are often the basis for academic promotion and grant funding. A researcher's list of publications is an important measure of success, and determines how he or she is recognized in his or her field. There is little else you can do that will beef-up your resume more than a good list of peer-reviewed published works in well-established scholarly journals.

There are many facets to being a scientist, but publication is a necessary one, and without it, a scientist's greatest achievements will go unnoticed. It is on record that when a young researcher asked Michael Faraday, the great physicist, the secret of his success as a scientific investigator, he replied, "The secret is comprised in three words—Work, Finish, Publish."

We've all heard the philosophical question, "If a tree falls in a forest and no one is around to hear it, does it make a sound?" We can also pose the question, "If an experiment is conducted in the lab and is not published, is it science?" Maybe. But it won't advance knowledge in the field, and it won't advance you in academia.

So, it is clear. You must publish. And not just publish, but publish in **peer-reviewed** journals. The process of peer review is the rigorous scrutiny of a scientist's scholarly work by other scientists in the same field. Peer review is the hallmark of scientific research.

Many would argue that the research endeavor has become mired by the demand on scientists to publish ever more papers. It is common for top scientists to have a publication list numbering in the hundreds. But how much does these prolific authors advance science is a subject of discussion. As Otto Loewi, the pharmacologist who discovered acetylcholine sarcastically pointed out: "A drug is a substance which, if injected into a rabbit, produces a paper." We must be careful not to let the pressure to publish dictate all of our research. There is much research that is worth pursuing, even if it does not ultimately yield a ton of papers.

Even Albert Einstein was caught up in the pressures of the publish-or-perish dogma. It was only after his impressive publication of five papers in 1905 that he was appointed as professor of physics at Zurich University. Further, it would not have been possible for him to publish these papers had it not been for the publications of other scientists before him who had also pondered the secrets of the universe.

Few of us will come anywhere near the brilliant publication of Einstein's 1905 remarkable papers. However, one thing is for certain—publishing important research results is one of the most important endeavors of any scientist.

The Top 8 Reasons to Publish Peer-Reviewed Research Papers

- The act of putting your research to paper will help you clarify your goals for the research, will help you in reviewing and interpreting your own data and force you to compare your work with that of others.
- Peer review gives you important feedback on the validity of your research approach, and can provide insight on next steps for advancing and interpreting your work.
- Communicating the information that you have found will help other researchers advance their work, thus building on the body of knowledge that exists in your field.
- Writing and publishing puts your research into larger context.
- Your published paper can help in the public understanding of a research question.
- Having a robust body of published works helps advance your career as you are considered for academic appointments and promotions.
- Publishing helps establish you as an expert in your field of knowledge.
- Peer-reviewed publication provides evidence that helps in the evaluation of merit of research funding requests.

Points to remember from Chapter 1

- Researchers must become writers. As researchers progress in their careers, their work demands higher levels of written output. Researchers must write grant proposals to fund their research, and research papers to support grant proposal ideas.

- Peer review is the hallmark of scholarly research work. A peer-reviewed research paper is a manuscript written by a scientist or scientists that details the results of a research study and that has been scrutinized and deemed of good quality by other scientists in the field.

- Publication of scientific articles, especially original research articles, is a necessary step in every scientist's academic career. The phrase "Publish or Perish" is often used to describe the pressure to publish research in academia.

- Principal investigators need their students and fellows to conduct the research to support the lab while they write because only a small percentage of grants submitted actually get funded, thus increasing the number of grant proposals that need to be written by principal investigators.

- Few principal investigators have time to teach students and fellows how to write research articles efficiently, and most graduate schools do not provide much training on writing and publishing research articles.

- Scientific research must be published in order for it to serve its purpose of building knowledge in the field of study.

Additional resources

Newport, Carl. *So Good They Can't Ignore You: Why skills trump passion in the quest for work you love.* Hachette Book Group, New York, 2012.

Exercise 1: Career goals

Think about your career in science thus far, and ask yourself the following questions:

EXAMPLE QUESTIONS AND ANSWERS:

Today's date:	
Question	**Answer**
What is your main area of research expertise?	*Local and global issues in children's environmental health research and training.*
What work are you best known for in your field?	*Studies that showed that rates of asthma are highest among minority and low-income populations that also have disparities in exposure to environmental pollutants.*
What is the main goal of your current research?	*To develop computational methods to mine big databases for further evidence on how environmental pollutants affect children's health.*
What is your next goal for academic promotion or advancement in your career?	*To receive faculty award for academic and mentoring excellence.* *To be named to the National Academy of Sciences.*
What do you need to do to achieve this goal?	*To publish three papers in top tier journals.* *Create an effective online course.* *Mentor 10 students and 2 postdoctoral fellows* *Receive one additional RO1 grant*
When will you accomplish this career goal?	*Month/Year*

Exercise 1: Career goals

Think about your career in science thus far, and ask yourself the following questions:

QUESTIONS TO BE ANSWERED BY YOU:

Today's date:	
Question	**Answer**
What is your main area of research expertise?	
What work are you best known for in your field thus far?	
What is the main goal of your current research?	
What is your next goal for academic promotion or advancement in your career?	
What do you need to do to achieve this goal?	
When will you accomplish your next career goal?	

You may go to www.drluzclaudio.com and download the forms for the following exercises, which you will be able to customize to fill in.

Chapter 2: It's All About the Data

"You can have data without information, but you cannot have information without data."

– **Daniel Keys Moran**, American computer programmer and science fiction writer.

Data are the results of any type of research activity that you perform as a scientist which gives you information about the scientific question that you are aiming to answer with your work. Data is the evidence that you have accumulated in your research, and data is what you will write about in your research papers.

Your data can be experimental, observational or descriptive. It can be quantitative or qualitative. It can arise from your original experiments, or from your re-analysis of the work of others.

The data that accumulates as a result of your research need to be analyzed, organized, interpreted and illustrated before it goes into your research paper. Because this workbook is intended for a broad range of research scientists, I will not talk about here about how to analyze or interpret data. Analysis and interpretation of data depend on the type of data that your research generates and the context provided by the existing literature.

The type of analysis that you perform will depend on the type of data that you have collected. ***Quantitative data*** is best analyzed through statistical methods. Techniques for ***qualitative data*** analysis (such as analyzing results of focus groups, open-ended questions on surveys, etc.) involves other methods of analysis such as grouping and sorting in order to detect patterns or differences among groups. Qualitative data analysis sometimes involves assigning values to different outcomes in order to turn it into quantifiable information.

Regardless of the type of data that your work has generated, for the purpose of producing a publishable research paper, you will need to sort through its meaning in order to illustrate your results in cohesive ways that can be understood by other scientists. Being meticulous in organizing your data is particularly important at this stage.

One issue that often arises is that experiments and observations may not have been conducted in a sequential manner. As it sometimes happens, you may do an experiment that presents more questions than answers. Another common problem in gathering your data is that some of the information required to complete a full research paper may have been done by other researchers in your laboratory, some of whom may have moved on to other jobs. If you find yourself in these kinds of situations, do not despair. We all go through the same challenges.

For now, just focus on gathering your data. Look at it with the aim of finding what it might be saying. Ask yourself, your colleagues, or your adviser if this set of data can be developed into a full story. To do that, it is best to start by organizing and illustrating the data in a way that can be more easily shared with knowledgeable colleagues.

Organizing your data

Most researchers learn by doing. Sure, we go to classes during graduate school. In class, we learn the basics and theories behind the scientific disciplines that we are studying. But it is in the lab or in the field where we actually collect data, where we really learn to *do* science. It is in only this *doing* of research science where the data collected becomes the substance for research papers.

It is extremely important to periodically take stock of the data that you have collected, review it, and assess its validity and meaning. The data will talk to you if you ask the right questions, do the right analyses, and are able to infer from those results the knowledge that is important to communicate in your papers. Of course, this is easier said than done. A good portion of data interpretation will be made easier by organizing the data in the most logical ways.

Before you try to explain your data to others, you must understand it yourself. Nothing will help you more to understand your data than illustrating it so you can visualize any patterns that may emerge. You may often find yourself overloaded with numbers. In cases such as this, graphing those numbers may be the only way to see the relationships. Sometimes real discoveries are made only after graphing and visualizing the data.

Methods for data visualization, illustration, and interpretation are beyond the scope of this book. You will learn most of those skills by doing research and trial and error. Even after many years of experience in research, I still have to do several versions of my data illustrations until I'm sure that they convey most clearly the results of my work. I will, however, give you a short overview of the kinds of illustrations that are most often used to prepare data for presentation or publication.

Illustrating your data

The types of graphics you choose will depend on the type of information you want to present. Choosing the right graphic will bring your data to life and make it easy for readers to comprehend your findings at a mere glance.

Please note that here we are only presenting an overview of some common rules of thumb for illustrating data. There are many other more comprehensive about the art and science of creating illustrations for different kinds of data.

Some of this information is somewhat logical, and the rest will come from reading the literature in your field, which will familiarize you with the way in which other scientists tend to illustrate similar types of data. A lot of this knowhow will come to you through the doing, the living and breathing your research and your data. Use your years of accumulated knowledge to present your results to the world in the best possible light so they can be clearly seen and interpreted by those lucky souls who get to read your paper.

Note that the overview presented below includes examples of different figure types. These are for illustration only, and do not necessarily represent real research results.

Tables

Tables show your readers the precise value of your data, and are especially useful when you have large amounts of data to present. Tables should include columns and rows that are clearly labeled, and must include the value units for the data presented.

Generally, it has become customary to put the variable that you purposely change (the independent variable) on the far left column and the measured (dependent variable) in the next columns. If your data includes several trials of the same experiment or observation, these can be given in each subsequent column, or as the mean (or average) and standard deviations or upper and lower limits of the different trials or observations.

You may also have a last column or row that totals, averages or in some way summarizes the different measurements. This last row or column is called a *derived quantity* or *derived value* because it arises from the different primary measures.

Clearly label rows and columns, and align the data properly so the table is neatly and logically arranged. Use only horizontal lines to separate column headings from the data. Table titles should be placed on top of the table, while explanatory footnotes should appear below. Add captions to explain what the table is intended to convey.

You can also use symbols to highlight some of the table results. For example, you may label results that show a statistically significant difference by marking those with an asterisk.

When using tables, some of the common mistakes to avoid are:

• Failing to label values. Label every value in the table by using appropriate headings in the columns and rows that clearly identify each group of values.

• Failing to provide units of measure for all values. Be careful when you have different units of measure within the same table. For example, using percentages and absolute numbers in the same columns without properly distinguishing the two can cause confusion, taking away from the usefulness of the data.

• Having too many columns, rows or footnotes. This may be an indication that your data is too complex for a single table. Consider presenting your data in more than one table.

 Tips for creating effective tables

1. Use a descriptive title (note that the blue table below has no title).

2. Avoid unnecessary columns or rows. For example, the column labeled "number" in the blue table is the same for all the values. Instead, define what N is in a footnote below the table, or in the table title (as shown in the example below)

3. Include value units such as percent, years, kilograms, etc.

4. Use footnotes to provide additional information or definitions.

5. Include p values or any other relevant information f statistical analyses were conducted.

Example of a table for a (fictitious) study of how diet affects weight loss differently in smokers and nonsmokers.

	Number	Mean Weight Loss	Smokers	Age	Diet
Group A	100	2.6	5.3	38.3	55
Group B	100	2.1	17.5	42.7	9
Group C	100	2.8	20.1	40.5	29
Group D	100	0.1	20.2	41.5	7

Table 1: Baseline characteristics of study group participants (N=100 for each group)

	Non-smokers	Non-smokers Diet	Smokers	Smokers Diet
Mean Age (years)	38.3	42.7	40.5	41.5
Percent on Diet*	55	9	29	7
Mean weight loss (Kg)**	2.6	2.1	2.8	0.1
Percent who lost weight***	5.3	17.5	20.1	20.2

* p< 0.05

**Kilograms of weight loss two weeks after intervention

**Current smoker defined as tobacco use within the last 30 days

Graphs and Charts

Trends and comparisons between variables are interpreted more clearly when presented as a figure rather than as a table. There are some general rules to follow when creating figures, for instance:

- Each axis should be clearly labeled

- Figure captions should appear underneath the figure

- Be mindful of extra charges by the journals, who may not always use color printing. If possible, use shades that can be distinguished when printed in black and white.

- Ensure that the scales used for the axes are appropriate and consistent throughout the figure

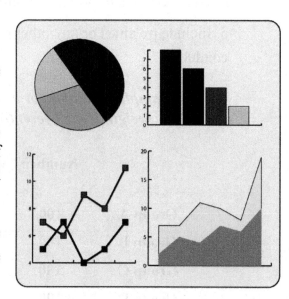

Figure 1: Types of graphs

Most importantly, you will need to decide which type of chart or graph best represents your data. The most common graphics used to display data include:

- Scatter plots
- Line graphs
- Bar charts
- Pie charts

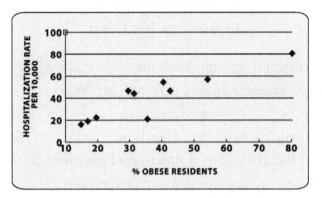

Figure 2: A Scatter Plot

Scatter plots

Scatter plots are most often used to illustrate a relationship (or lack thereof) between two variables: typically an independent and a dependent variable. The independent variable should be plotted on the x-axis, and the dependent variable on the y-axis. Each axis should be properly labeled and must include the units used for each measure.

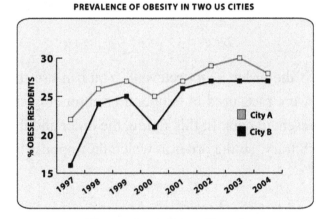

Figure 3: A Line Graph

Line graphs

Line graphs are a great way to illustrate any *trends* in your data, especially if those trends have been measured over time. These trends might go unnoticed if the data were presented in table format. One important thing to remember with line graphs is to make sure that your axes are scaled properly so they provide an accurate illustration of the data.

It is also important to note that as you connect the dots in a line graph, you assume that the time between your measurements followed a straight line in between the measured points. So for instance, Figure 3 shows that during the months between 1997 and 1998, there was a smooth and steep increase in the percentage of obese residents in City A. However, this may not have been the case. It is possible that the data increase occurred in a different way—perhaps a sudden jump or a bumpy climb. Keep this in mind as you decide whether a line graph is the best way to showcase your data, and whether the intervals you use for the x and y axis are appropriately spaced to best show your data points.

Bar charts

If your data is discrete and you wish to explore trends or compare between different groups, you should use a bar chart. Bar charts can be presented using horizontal bars or vertical bars against properly scaled reference points. Although horizontal or vertical bar graphs may be used, it is important to note that vertical bars are more common in research papers.

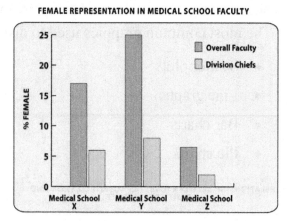

Figure 4: A Bar Chart

Bar charts are useful for presenting data from a single element measured in more than one experimental group. You may consider using a **clustered bar chart** if you wish to compare multiple variables among different groups.

For instance, in Figure 4, the *groups* are the medical schools. The figure *measures* the percentage of female faculty as a function of overall faculty and as a function of division chiefs. At a glance you can see the comparisons between the groups as well as between the clusters. One correction that I would make to this bar chart, however, is the order of the medical schools on the x axis. I would put Medical School Y first (closer to the 0) followed by Medical School X, and then Medical School Z, because aesthetically, it is often a good idea to organize the data in an ascending or descending pattern.

Keep in mind, however, that you can only do this if the order is not relevant. You can use the ascending to descending method unless the groups were measured in temporal or chronological order, or some other order that is important to the presented data. In this figure, the order and the labels of the Medical Schools as X, Y, and Z was arbitrary, so the order in which they appear on the x axis is unimportant.

Either way, you should aim for clarity and consistency in the presentation of your results. Once you decide how to order the data in your first figure, be sure to use the same order for all figures throughout the paper.

If the measures illustrated on a bar chart are composed of more than one observation, then the top of each bar should include error bars. The error bars denote the mean and standard deviations (or standard errors) obtained from the multiple measures of the same outcome. They can show whether the results between the groups are truly different (to a significant degree) because it is easy to see any overlap between the error bars.

Pie charts

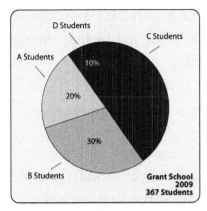

Figure 5: Pie Chart

Use a pie chart…or better, consider other options.

Pie charts are seldom used in the scientific literature. Perhaps a pie chart would be semi-appropriate if you were comparing parts of a whole (i.e., if your data adds up to 100%). The truth is, pie charts are less precise in representing your data. You may find use for them in poster or oral presentations, but most of the time, you should keep them out of your articles and reports.

If you insist on using a pie chart, be sure to use horizontal text labels. Start the largest slice at 12 o'clock, and go clockwise from larger to smaller slices. Be mindful of how much color you include, because many journals charge extra for color printing. Use pie charts sparingly, if at all.

Photographs

A picture is worth a thousand words. Or is it?

Although not appropriate in every circumstance, photographs can be a useful and powerful tool for presenting data. One of my favorite papers in the area of children's environmental health is by Guillette *et al* published in the journal *Environmental Health Perspectives* in 1998 (see figure 6).

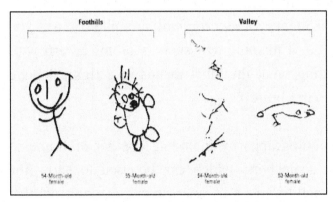

Figure 6: Photograph

The paper looked at the neurobehavioral effects of pesticide exposure in children in two villages in Mexico. The paper studied one group which was heavily exposed, and another that was not. The author included photographs of two drawings from two children in each village. The pictures are shocking in that they clearly show the huge difference in drawing abilities between children who were heavily exposed to pesticides compared to those who were not. Because the pictures accurately illustrate the results of the study, they serve as an appropriate and powerful tool for making the point of the paper very clear.

Photographs should only be used when they accurately represent the results of what you are trying to illustrate. If you are using a photograph to illustrate a typical result from your data, make sure that the photograph you include in the paper IS a representative example of the overall data. Photographs that represent an outlier measurement or a best-case scenario are misleading and should be avoided unless they are clearly labeled as such and include enough context so readers know that it is not representative of the overall data.

For example, the following types of photographs may be appropriate illustrations for research papers:

- Microscopy – To illustrate features on tissues or cells, or to show experimental outcomes using cell stains or procedures. For microscopic photographs, make sure to include a scale bar that includes the unit measure, usually in microns.
- Anatomy – To show an anatomical structure in relation to others or a specific feature. Use an object of known dimensions in the photograph so that readers can estimate the size of the object that is being presented. For instance, a ruler works well to show scale.
- Anthropology – To show the special characteristics of a group of people.
- Archeology – To indicate the location of an artifact found at an archeological site.
- Case studies – Photographs of patients with a particular lesion. Photographs of patients before and after treatment.

After you have selected a suitable photograph that accurately represents your results, you will need to properly highlight its important features. You can use labels, arrows, or any other indicator to point to any feature that you want to draw attention to. For example, it would be unwise to assume that every reader will be able to identify a *macrophage* in a photo. So if you are trying to show a macrophage, it's best to point to it in some way such as adding an arrow or labeling the cell with the letter "M", and indicating what the label means in a figure legend under the photograph. An example of this is shown in Figure 7.

You can also enhance useful information from photographs by including context or frame of reference. This can be accomplished by adding scale bars, which can be used to show the distance between two points; for example, in a satellite image or microscopic components that lack another frame of reference. This is not important if the photo already has an obvious frame of reference for the reader, such as a photograph of a leg showing a lesion, or a lab rat being held in someone's hand. When deciding whether a scale bar or a reference object is needed in the photograph, consider whether it will be important for the reader to have this frame of reference in order to understand the photograph.

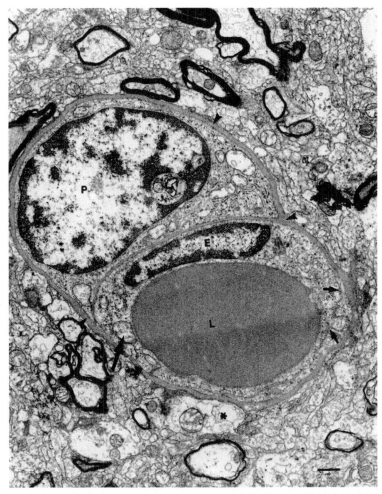

Figure 7: Micrograph

This is an electron micrograph of a human cerebral capillary also known as the blood-brain barrier. Note that the micrograph is properly labeled with large arrows (mitochondria), small arrows (tight junctions) and arrowheads (basement membrane). Also, different components are labeled with letters (L=capillary lumen, E=endothelial cell, P=pericyte). And a Scale bar is given at the bottom right (1micron). From Claudio *et al*, 1995)

Photographs also come with unique responsibilities. If your photograph includes a person or multiple persons, you must protect their privacy by making them unrecognizable. This can be achieved by blocking out the eye area, or by cropping the face out of the picture entirely. It is also imperative to obtain informed consent whenever human subjects are used in photographs.

 Rules for using photographs

- Accurately represent results of your study.

- Point to the important features using arrows or other labels.

- Use appropriate scale bars such as the measure of a micron in microscopy, a ruler in photography, or the distance for a kilometer on an aerial photograph.

- Protect people's privacy. Avoid including identifiable features.

Diagrams, Drawings and Screen Captures

Sometimes it is helpful to the reader if the author includes a diagrammatic representation of some of the information that is being conveyed in the paper. Some types of information that you might consider including as a diagram or drawing are line drawings of anatomical structures, diagrams of molecules, flow-charts of procedures and other examples of key information that is hard to put into words or that is better explained with a visual representation.

Screen captures can be used to describe a computerized product that is being discussed or used in the study[1].

Online publication has made it possible for some journals to allow authors to include supplemental materials with their papers. Oftentimes, these kinds of illustrations may not be part of the paper per se, but may be included as supplemental material that may enhance the experience of reading the paper for those interested in more in-depth or in additional information.

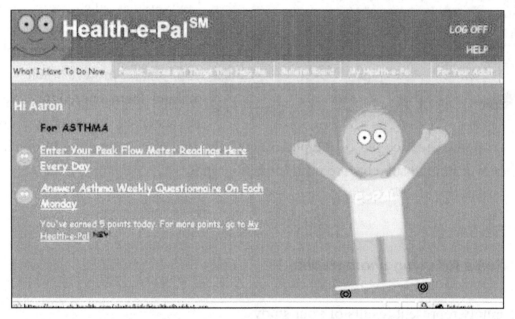

Figure 8: Screen capture. From: Arnold RJG, Stingone JA, Claudio L 2012

Maps

Like photographs, maps can be powerful tools for illustrating your data. They can be used whenever geography or location is a noteworthy part of the study. For instance, I had completed a study of the correlation between socioeconomic factors and asthma hospitalization rates throughout New York City. Although I had calculated hospitalization rates for all the neighborhoods and correlation coefficients for their relationship with SES, nothing was more powerful than two side-by-side maps—one showing median household income by neighborhood and the other showing asthma hospitalization rates by neighborhood (see figure 8).

---

[1] For privacy reasons, it is important that no real data is depicted in the screen capture.

Whenever I gave a presentation on this topic, people would gasp when they saw that the same areas were shaded on the two maps. The New York Times published the maps on its front page. Communities mobilized using the maps, and health policymakers took action to address the issue. Maps can be great for illustrating these kind of data.

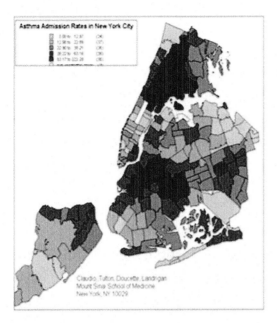 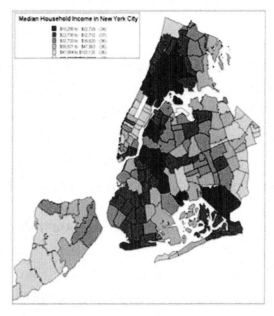

Figure 8: Maps. From Claudio *et al*, 1999

Maps can be created using geographic information systems (GIS), which is software used to analyze and display data on spatial or geographical representations. It can be purchased with map templates for different areas, or customized as needed. If you decide to use GIS-generated maps, make sure that the template accurately represents your geographic units, such as zip codes, districts, counties, states, census tracks, etc.

Keep in mind that depending on the nature of your data, a map could unknowingly make individuals, areas or communities identifiable. This may or may not be in violation of protections for human subjects, so check with your Institutional Review Board to see if this is acceptable for your kind of data.

Using the Figures to Guide the Writing of your Research Paper

As you work to create the right illustrations of your data for your paper, keep in mind that your illustrations must stand alone; they need to convey the results without the reader having to consult additional information or make additional calculations. Each illustration, regardless of its type, should present a complete result that can be deduced from just examining the illustration and reading its title, captions, labels and any other features within the illustration itself.

In order to get used to the idea of presenting compelling figures, I tell my trainees to work from the data illustrations when writing their papers, and to keep the raw data in separate files. In this way, I want them to get used to the idea of describing the results based on those figures, just as the intended readers will do when the paper is published. Writing from the figures and tables will also help you focus on writing instead of thinking about doing other analyses and experiments.

Of course, this does not mean that once you have created your figures for the paper that you will not need the raw data anymore. Of course, you will often need to refer to the raw data in the process of writing for publication. For instance, reviewers may ask you to provide additional analyses or present other evidence. In addition, institutional compliance requires that raw data be kept for a number of years. Always check your institutional guidelines before you destroy any of the original data used writing the paper.

Important Notice About the Responsible Conduct of Research

Responsible conduct of research is defined by the National Institutes of Health as "the practice of scientific investigation with integrity. It involves the awareness and application of established professional norms and ethical principles in the performance of all activities related to scientific research."

To ensure that ethical principles are being followed, research institutions are required to have committees charged with the review of protocols for research proposed by its investigators. These committees review any research involving human subjects, Institutional Review Board (IRB) or involving laboratory animals, Institutional Animal Care and Use Committee (IACUC).

Most reputable journals now require that each author attest that his or her research has been reviewed and approved by the appropriate committee at their institution. Failure to comply with either of these committees' assessments can result in very serious consequences to researchers. Responsible conduct of research training is mandatory at all institutions that receive federal funding. Beyond that, you should care about whether your research protocols comply with fundamental ethical guiding principles for how to treat study participants.

Please ensure that you—as well as any colleagues involved in your research project—understand all the requirements regarding the ethical use of research subjects (human or animal), and that all relevant conditions have been met prior to conducting your research. Failure to do so from the very beginning of the research project will potentially invalidate your data, rendering it unpublishable.

The American Psychological Association has published a list of nine areas that comprise the responsible conduct of research. I reproduce these here because I find their format serves as a mental checklist for investigators to review if they are complying with ethical conduct of research requirements. You can also find these at: http://www.apa.org/research/responsible/

Checklist Of Areas Important In The Responsible Conduct Of Research (RCR)
From the American Psychological Association

Collaborative Science: Collaborations take place in a variety of forms, including the borrowing and lending of supplies, resources and equipment between researchers; seeking input from an expert in a different discipline; and partnering with colleagues who have a similar background or field of knowledge for fresh ideas and abilities.

Conflicts of Interest and Commitments: Conflicts of interests or commitments are not inherently negative; rather, the way in which the conflict is managed is important.

Data Acquisition, Management, Sharing and Ownership: This site is designed as a central location for viewing and retrieving shared data archives relevant to psychological science.

Human Research Protections: Research with human participants plays a central role in advancing knowledge in the biomedical, behavioral and social sciences.

Lab Animal Welfare: APA has and continues to support efforts to improve laboratory animal welfare through the implementation of policies and regulations that both maintain the integrity of scientific research and sustain the welfare of such animals.

Mentoring: Mentoring a less-experienced researcher is a professional responsibility of all scientists. The ultimate goal of the mentor is to establish the trainee as an independent researcher.

Peer Review: Positive peer reviews contribute to increased funding opportunities, academic advancement and a good reputation.

Publications Practices and Responsible Authorship: Although researchers can disseminate their findings through many different avenues, results are most likely to be published as an article in a scholarly journal.

Research Misconduct: Institutions should have procedures in place to investigate and when appropriate report findings of misconduct to the Office of Research Integrity (ORI). They should also have policies that protect both whistleblowers and the accused until a determination is made.

Points to remember from Chapter 2

- The result of research is data. Data, whether quantitative or qualitative should be of sufficient quality and significance to allow for the scientist to draw conclusions that can be expressed in a research paper.

- The researcher must find the best ways to express the data in a visual format so that readers can grasp the information being presented.

- You should work directly from the data figures that will be used to illustrate the paper. The raw data that was used to create the figures should be stored elsewhere, and should only be consulted when needed.

- Figures and tables that are used for a paper should be self-contained and should include everything that the reader needs to understand the research results. Thus, the figures and tables should include any legends that will help the reader understand the data.

- All data must be generated through the ethical conduct of research. Prior to the conduct of the research project, study protocols must be reviewed and approved by the appropriate institutional review boards that regulate the use of humans or animals in research.

Additional resources:

Nussbaumer Knaflic, Cole. *Storytelling with Data*. Wiley 2015

Data visualization software:

- https://datawrapper.de – Software to create line or bar graphs, maps, donut graphs and tables from data you copy/paste onto its easy interface.

- www.charted.co – Software useful for creating bar graphs of publically-available data. Automatically updates your charts every 30 minutes based on any changes in the database, using a link you provide.

- www.raw.densitydesign.org – Lets you copy/paste your data to create vector-based visualizations using a library of customizable formats.

Important! The open source data visualization tools listed above is not an exhaustive list. Please note that it is YOUR responsibility to ensure data security. If your data includes identifiable information from study participants, you will need to remove identifiers before entering your data into a software program.

Exercise 2: *Getting to know your data*

For this exercise, gather the results of your studies thus far. What do your results mean? Think about assembling your results into a cohesive, meaningful story. What does your data say? Note that in this table the word "experiment" refers to whatever activity you perform to make research observations, whether it is laboratory-based, population-based, interventional or observational.

Example: Paper on Asthma Prevalence Rates and Socioeconomic Status

	Experiment	Main observation	Secondary observations	Type of graphic
General ↓	*Analysis of hospital reports on hospitalization rates by borough and census data*	*Bronx had highest rates, and is the borough with lowest household income*	*Most hospitalizations in children under 17 years old.* *Other boroughs had similar rates*	*Table of rates by borough*
↓	*Analysis of hospitalization rates by zip code*	*Zip codes with high minority populations had highest hospitalization rates*	*Hospitalization rates higher than any in literature* *Low income/minority neighborhoods most affected*	*Table with correlation coefficients*
↓ **Specific**	*Asthma hospitalization rates, household income and % of minority populations by quintiles*	*Co-localization of low income, high asthma rates and high minority populations in the same zip codes*	*Clustering of high asthma rates in certain geographic areas of the Bronx and Brooklyn*	*Maps of hospitalization rates and income rates colored by quintile*

You may go to www.drluzclaudio.com and download the forms for the following exercises, which you will be able to customize to fill in.

Exercise 2: Getting to know your data

Fill out this table for your own data. Add rows as needed.

Date:	Experiment	Main observation	Secondary observations	Type of graphic
General ↓				
↓				
↓				
↓				
Specific				

Chapter 3: Is Your Data Ready for Primetime?

"People who think they know everything are a great annoyance to those of us who do."

– Isaac Asimov, American scientist and author of popular science books

As with any task, getting ready and preparing your materials before you start are key to your success. Before you begin any journey, you decide what will be your destination. You get a map and make a plan for the route you will take. You pack your bags. If you find that there's something else you need, you go buy it. Only after much preparation and planning do you take the first step.

In just the same way, writing a research article will take some planning and organization. To start, you need to know what you will be writing about. This should be clearly delineated in a good title. The title not only tells your readers what your paper is all about, but it will also tell YOU what to include and what to exclude from the writing.

In this chapter you will learn how to hone your message and focus on what you want to communicate about your work. Here, you will choose your "destination", the specific theme or topic of your paper, which will be articulated in your title. You will determine whether your data is ready for publication and decide what data will be <u>in</u> and what will be <u>out</u>. In the next chapter, you will create an outline—the roadmap that will take you to your destination.

Are you ready?

Writing a working title

In order to get organized, you need to focus on what you intend to accomplish. A great first step to help you do that is to write a working title! Yes. Nothing helps you more when zeroing-in on your intention than giving it a concise, specific and well-defined name that delineates the content you intend to write.

A good working title should be a concise statement of exactly what will be included in the paper. The title is a label that specifically and clearly states the contents of the paper.

Although the title accomplishes a description of the paper with an economy of words, it should be long enough to capture the essence of the investigation and give the readers enough information to decide whether or not they are interested in reading further.

Although it seems logical to start from the beginning, the title is much more than just the beginning of your paper.

Writing a good title will help you to identify the main subject of your paper and focus on which key findings to include. This will tell your brain that you need to focus solely on what should be contained in the paper based on the title that you have composed.

Any points, ideas, thoughts, or data that stray beyond what the title describes should be left out of the paper and should be put aside when you are focused on writing THIS paper.

Do not make the mistake of overreaching with your working title. Your paper should concentrate on a specific aspect of your research that can adequately be supported by relevant data. It should have one main idea that is supported by the results that you plan to incorporate.

At this point in your writing process, you should only use this draft of the title as a focal point to help you concentrate on what you want to accomplish with your manuscript. Some journals may have character limits on the title, but this is nothing to concern yourself with now; you can always shorten the title later if necessary. Remember, the working title is a tool to help YOU focus and plan.

It is very likely that after you have written the paper, you will go back and revise the original draft title. In this final step, you will ask, "Does this title adequately reflect what I have written?" (An example of just this kind of

---

Evolution of a Working Title

Suppose you work with a community-based organization serving primarily African-American communities. You conduct studies on a wide range of issues that affect the community including asthma, education, prostate cancer, breast cancer and hypertension. You and your colleagues have collected massive amounts of data on community-based interventions, and you want to publish your results.

One way to begin is by choosing one of the studies that has the most complete set of results. Put aside everything else for now, and write a title that reflects the work that you have decided to focus on for THIS paper.

Here is the evolution of a title as an example. Notice how it becomes more specific without necessarily detailing the results or conclusions of the study.

- *Study of Breast Cancer in Minority Women*

- *Study of Breast Cancer in African American Women*

- *Study of Breast Cancer in African American Women in Harlem, New York*

- *Community-based Intervention on Breast Cancer Screening in African American Women Living in Harlem, New York*

After completing the paper, perhaps you notice that there is actually a sizable number of Hispanic and Asian women in your study and that your data shows strong effectiveness. You decide to change the final title to "Effective Community-based Intervention on Breast Cancer Screening in Minority Women Living in Harlem, New York."

situation is given in the box "Evolution of a working title").

If the answer is yes, then you have done a great job staying focused. If the answer is no, you may have deviated from your original intention and may want to go back to revise the content or amend the original title if needed.

 Once you have a working title, type it and post it somewhere visible in your work area as a reminder of your writing goal.

Data readiness

After writing your title, ask yourself, "Do I have enough data to write a complete story about this topic?"

Even if you have presented abstracts of your research work at scientific conferences, you will know that writing an abstract and writing a full-length research paper are two different beasts. Producing a conference abstract and presenting it at a conference are only a fraction of what writing a paper will be.

What this means is that even though presenting at a conference will give you a sense of the state of your data, input from other peers and a taste of peer-review, it will only prepare you for writing the paper, and should not be taken as the only indicator of data-readiness.

In trying to answer the question, "Is this data ready for submission to a peer-reviewed research journal?" there are at least three possible answers to this question, which reminds me of the story of Goldilocks.

Too little data

The main question for you to ask yourself is:

"Does the set of observations that you have collected for this paper constitute enough evidence to support an important conclusion related to the topic of the working title?"

It's possible to begin writing your paper before collecting all the data, but it is important to consider that any future data may contradict, strengthen or change your interpretation of previous results, which may change your conclusions. How likely is this? If it's a possibility, you may find yourself needing to rewrite important sections based on this new evidence—that is, if you begin before this data is collected. This is okay, and may even be part of the thrill of discovery. <u>Do not put off writing just because you have not yet collected enough data.</u>

Writing based on what data you have—even with this limited data—will help clarify your work, will give you clues as to what your next steps should be in your research and will give you some material that you will be able to discuss with colleagues for receiving input.

Don't let this lack of data stop you from writing.

If you don't have enough data for a full paper, consider conducting the experiments or collecting the data that will make this particular scholarly work complete. A good outline can be a useful tool for pointing out what data you may still need to collect to make this paper a full and cohesive story.

 If you find that you don't have enough data for a full paper, write anyway. The act of writing will help you find the next steps to follow to for your research.

Too much data

Did you collect so much data that you are overwhelmed with results that point to many conclusions? Too much data can seem like a blessing, but be careful not to create a mega paper that may be overwhelming.

If you have too much data, consider dividing the data into more than one paper, and focus on a single aspect of the data in order to be able to write a cohesive and concise story.

For example, one of my students collected data on respiratory health in several large communities. Because of the extensive database that was generated and the large and diverse number of participants, writing only one paper to incorporate all of the important findings proved to be unwieldy. Thus, we decided to divide the data into two papers: one showing the results in adults and the other in children.

Dividing the data into more than one paper can be a solution in certain situations, but it's important not to overdo it to the point that you end up with too many tiny papers.

A good rule of thumb is that your paper should have enough data to support one or two main conclusions, and no more than four additional key observations. More than that can be too confusing for the reader, and should be in a second or even a third publication.

Just right? Then write!

If you have the right amount of data for a paper, start focused writing now! Remember, the rate of discovery has become so fast-paced that papers are constantly being published in your field. If you start writing and then stop to collect more data, you will have to update the writing you have already completed in order to incorporate relevant new literature, delaying your publication even further.

The bottom line is this: Write if you have too little data. Write if you have too much data. If you have a complete set of data results that constitutes a publishable research paper, <u>you must start focusing on writing it right now</u>!

Getting input from collaborators regarding data readiness

It is the rare researcher who works independently and is a sole author of a research paper. Most researchers work in teams and rely on each other for different parts of the research project.

Even after working in this field for almost 30 years, there always seems to be someone whose expertise is more extensive than mine in a certain area of work, or whose opinion would be helpful when preparing a paper for publication. Sometimes all you need is another set of eyes to look at your results with a different perspective to better explain or interpret a complex set of findings.

I rarely submit a paper without some input from colleagues or collaborators. You may solicit input at many stages of the writing process, from making your figures and tables all the way to the final draft for submission. You may approach different people at different stages to request input on specific questions or guidance on certain aspects of your paper. Some ways in which you can request input from your community are outlined below.

Consult advisors and coauthors

You should work collaboratively with your coauthors on the paper, especially during the beginning stages of planning the paper, and at the end when you are making the final edits. *Make sure that you have the approval of every contributor, and that they are aware of your intention to prepare the data for publication.*

At the beginning of the process, once I have figures and tables that are close to final, I like to informally present them to collaborators. At this point, I am looking for their input on interpreting the results. It is helpful to show a graph and ask your chosen collaborate what they think of the findings. Does this figure show the data in its best, most clear way?

Coauthors must be in agreement regarding the data to be published, and they must share your interpretation of the data. In fact, journals require that all authors provide signed statements regarding their role in the paper as well as an acknowledgement that they agree to the publication of the work. For this reason, it is important to gain consensus from all coauthors before you start writing in earnest.

That said, my experience has been that research papers do not get written by committee. Someone has to take the lead in actually writing the first drafts. I advise you to consult the coauthors when you have collected the data and created the figures and figure legends. Then, discuss with them the results obtained and the potential conclusions that you may derive from them. Following this, you can write the first draft (yourself). You can request further input after you have the draft complete.

Present at a professional conference

When you present your preliminary work at a scientific conference, you have the opportunity to compare your work with colleagues in your field. You may also ask questions of other experts and get ideas for additional experiments. The experience will make you more aware about how your work compares with that of other scientists. See Chapter 4 for more information about presenting at professional conferences.

Read papers that closely resemble what you are doing

You must keep current on the latest literature in your area of study. Period. This may seem overwhelming when literature advances so fast in many fields, or it may seem difficult if your work is particularly novel or original, in which case there might not be a lot of published material in your specific area of work.

Keep in mind that scientific research builds on the work of others, so you are likely to find papers that are similar in content, topic or methods to your own. Read these papers carefully and determine how your planned work compares. Ask yourself: "Can I provide enough information that will add new knowledge to the field?"

Give a Works-In-Progress Seminar

Your academic department may have a forum for researchers to present their ongoing work informally. Take advantage of it. Presenting your work to your colleagues in an informal setting can be an excellent opportunity for collecting ideas that could strengthen your paper.

If you get critiqued, don't get discouraged or take it personally. This is a good thing. Listen with an open mind to the colleagues who critique your presentation. This will help you to create a much stronger research plan, and your papers will be much more robust as you prepare them for journal submission. Ask the audience at the end of your presentation if the paper is ready to submit to a journal, or if there is anything else that can be done to make this data ready for writing into a research paper.

Seek one-on-one consultation with an expert

Approaching an expert scientist who is outside of your immediate circle of collaborators and co-workers can be very intimidating. Most of those VIPs don't have the time to review your work, much less, to give you feedback.

One key to approaching a guru in your field is to let them know WHY you are asking for their opinion. It may be that your work is closely related to theirs, and so the findings may be of interest to them. Try to think about what is in it for them. Why should they take the time to look at your data? Be honest, specific and direct with your request. For instance, saying something like:

"I have obtained these results in my latest experiments. Given your extensive experience in this field, I would like your opinion of the results in figure 3, especially in light of your own findings in your related paper from 2013, which served as inspiration for my experiments. Your opinion will be very valuable to me as I prepare these data for publication."

If you have an expert who you respect and who knows your research area fairly well, consider asking him or her to look at your results and outline (see how to write an outline, below). Choose a person who is an experienced author—perhaps someone who has participated as a journal reviewer or a member of a journal editorial board. This person will be able to advise you on whether you have collected enough data to write a paper for submission to a scientific journal and will have an opinion on the interpretation of the results.

It is not necessary to have every kind of input in order to successfully prepare your data for publication. The only people who you must consult early and thoroughly at different stages of your writing are your collaborators, especially your coauthors. However, if you do have people who can serve as resources for preparing your data, it will be very helpful as you move along in your work.

 You are ready to focus on writing a research paper, if...

- You have enough evidence to substantiate a cohesive conclusion.
- You have obtained feedback from colleagues. You may have received this feedback at a conference after presenting an abstract, poster or oral presentation, or maybe after presenting at an internal seminar, lecture or work-in-progress presentation. It may even be after presenting the work informally at a whiteboard.
- You have consulted your collaborators, and they all agree that the data is ready for publication.
- You have found similar papers in the literature that have a similar number of data points.

Points to remember from Chapter 3

- Writing a working title helps you to focus on what you should include in the paper, and importantly, to determine what should be excluded.

- Having too few data points for a full paper should not stop you from starting to draft a paper. The act of writing will help you determine what other experiments you may need to conduct to generate enough data for a paper.

- When you have too much data, you should consider splitting it into more than one. Having too much data in a paper can make it confusing and unwieldy. As a rule of thumb, aim to write a research paper that has one or two main conclusions and no more than four supporting additional key observations.

- Present your preliminary work at institutional forums such as work-in-progress seminars to gage the response to your data and request input on your work.

- Consult your advisors and coauthors early in the process of data collection and planning for a research paper. You can also seek consultation from an expert by consulting their opinion on a specific area of your work.

- When preparing a work-in-progress seminar, organize it in a similar format as a research paper with an Introduction, Methods, Results and Conclusions sections. Elicit specific comments from the audience and request feedback on the interpretation of results, the data visualization methods used and any other aspect of the work.

Exercise 3: Data readiness to-do list

Think about the dataset that you worked on in the previous chapter. Use this to-do list to get your data ready for publication and keep track of input that you receive from colleagues and collaborators.

Example of Paper (for illustration purposes only)

Working title: *Effective Community-based Intervention on Breast Cancer Screening in Minority Women Living in Harlem, New York*

Main conclusions:

1. Video demonstrations of the process of mammography help demystify the test and increase rates of mammography in minority women.

2. Video education is most effective when done by minority women from the community.

3. Video messaging should include information about the relationship of survival with early detection.

4. Effect of the educational intervention was independent of demographic variables.

Titles of figures and tables:

1. Table: Demographics of the community and study population

2. Flowchart: Showing how intervention and control groups were created

3. Diagram: Storyboard of video-based intervention

4. Bar graph: Rates of mammography in intervention and control groups

5. Table: Showing that income and education did not affect mammography rates

---

List of collaborators, roles

Name	Role
Dr. Mentor	*Principal Investigator*
Dr. New Kid on the Block	*Provided demographic analysis*
Ms. Student #1	*Collected data on African Americans*
Mr. Student #2	*Collected data on Hispanics*
Ms. Director of community organization	*Created video content, obtained consent*
Dr. Statistician	*Did all data analysis, created graph*

Colleagues consulted		
Name	**Date of meeting or email**	**Comments/follow up**
Dr. Mentor	*Meeting: date*	*Separate minority groups Acknowledge new grant*
Dr. New Kid	*Meeting: date*	*Compare data to reported rates by zip codes*
Ms. Student #1	*Email: date*	*Control for health insurance and income*
Mr. Student #2	*Email: date*	*No comments*
Ms. Director of community organization	*Meeting director and CBO staff on (date)*	*Do not include map of intervention sites*
Dr. Statistician	*Meeting: date*	*Need number of refusals*

Presentation	**Comments received**	**Follow up**
Works-in-progress seminar (date)	*Dr. Who had question about graph #4* *Dr. Pepper suggested comparing to data on intervention using pamphlets*	*Turned line graph into bar graph. Much clearer!* *Got the paper. Will add to discussion.*
Lab meeting	*Pat suggested adding nativity to demographic data*	*Added nativity data to Table 1*

You may go to www.drluzclaudio.com and download the forms for the following exercises, which you will be able to customize to fill in.

Exercise 3: Data readiness to-do list

Think about the dataset that you worked on in the previous chapter. Use this to-do list to get your data ready for publication and keep track of input that you receive from colleagues and collaborators. **Insert your data below**.

Working title:

Main conclusions:

Title of figures and tables: 1.   2.   3.   4.   5.

List of collaborators and roles	
Name	**Role**

Colleagues consulted:		
Name	**Date of meeting or email**	**Comments/follow up**

Presentations, comments, follow-up plans:		
Presentation	**Comments received**	**Follow up**

Chapter 4: Publishing Preliminary Data at Professional Conferences

"If I had to live my life again, I'd make the same mistakes, only sooner."
— Tallulah Bankhead, American actress

Even before getting your work ready for publication in peer-reviewed journals, you will have many opportunities to present your results at seminars, works-in-progress lectures and other venues in oral as well as print presentations. These are excellent opportunities for you to start honing your message and refining your research conclusions so they are most clearly understood by your peers. These kinds of presentations are also great opportunities for getting feedback and critique that may be helpful as you start putting together your research papers.

Most academic departments will have seminar series of lectures at which faculty, students and postdoctoral fellows can (or are required to) present their work. Take every opportunity to present your work in progress before putting together your research paper.

Consider organizing your presentations as you would a research paper, using the same general outline headings such as Background or Introduction, Materials and Methods, Results, Discussion, Conclusions. As you present, ask for advice from the audience. Come up with a list of specific questions to pose to your colleagues before your presentation. Ask for input at every stage of your presentation in order to get the most useful information to help you put together a research paper based on that presentation.

What are professional conferences?

Many scientific societies, journals and professional associations host conferences that consist of a number of activities, including preliminary study presentations. These professional conferences are meetings of scientists who work in the same general discipline, specialty or subspecialty. The purpose is to promote the exchange of ideas, debate topics important to the field, coordinate position statements of the group and/or serve as a venue for continuing education of its members.

One key feature is the presentation of current research. Often, these presentations are the first time the research study is presented outside of the institution where it was conducted. Conference presentations are great opportunities for showcasing your research results, receiving feedback, and finding out where your results fit in relation to the research conducted by your peers. Presenting at professional conferences is often considered a necessary first step to take towards peer-reviewed research publication.

While your ultimate goal is to publish original works in high-impact, peer-reviewed scientific journals, you might consider first presenting the preliminary research data in abstract form at conferences in order to further hone your message, obtain feedback from a broader audience of experts in your field, and contrast and compare your research with others who have done similar work.

Presenting at conferences is also an excellent opportunity for you to offer and receive comments on the research, as well as share ideas and experiences with colleagues. Professional conferences are exciting incubators for scientific debate, networking and meeting fellow scientists that share your interests. Submitting an abstract and presenting your research at a conference is an excellent way for you to gauge how other scientists may respond to your findings and can give you very good ideas on how to proceed with your research and your research paper.

Conference abstracts

Conference abstracts are summaries of presentations made by scientists at professional conferences. Typically, abstracts are short, ranging from 200 to 500 words. They should summarize very briefly the rationale, methods and results of the study, and end with one or two sentences describing the conclusions.

When you submit an abstract in response to a conference "call for presentations", it will be reviewed for relevance and professionalism. The level of scrutiny that your abstract will receive during the review for acceptance at a conference varies widely, and typically depends on a) the number of abstracts that are submitted versus the number of presentation spots available, b) the policies of the review committee, c) whether the abstracts are published in a journal's proceedings, d) the relevance of the abstract topic in relation to the main themes being presented at the conference, and e) other factors particular to the conference organizers.

If your work is accepted for presentation at a conference, you may be asked to show your work either in an oral presentation or on a poster. While some conferences may ask you to choose between presenting in oral or poster form, they may not always grant you your wish. Be flexible; both forms of presentations allow you to receive critical feedback from your peers and are excellent ways of improving your research.

Either way, oral or poster presentations are often a matter of preference. In terms of publication, conference organizers typically only publish the abstracts and not the full presentations.

Therefore, it hardly matters in which format you end up making a presentation at the actual conference.

Oral conference presentations

Seminars or lectures are forms of oral presentations. They have several formats such as the panel-style presentation (where multiple speakers share the stage simultaneously), the short presentation (10 minutes) or the long speech (20-60 minutes). Oral presentations are often accompanied by electronic slides, most often made with Microsoft PowerPoint.

Usually, large conferences group oral presentations into sessions by topic. Each session may be composed of a number of presentations on a particular topic, and may have a moderator to facilitate the discussion. If you are good on your feet and enjoy presenting in front of an audience, oral presentations at scientific conferences are an excellent way for you to gain exposure for your research, practice your public speaking skills and receive feedback that can be helpful for advancing your research work.

 Tips for great oral presentations

- First, decide what you know. Before you start putting together your presentation, make a list of the main points of your presentation. There should not be more than three. These are the things that you want people to remember after they have listened to you. Then organize your presentation around those points.

- Decide what it is that you don't know. To know what you don't know is in itself a form of wisdom. Be aware that it is understood that presentations at conferences are works in progress. It is okay to ask the audience for input. When giving oral presentations conferences, I sometimes include a slide with some of the questions that I am pondering as to how to best advance the research. Find a way to elicit ideas from the audience.

- Remember, you are the expert: If the thought of presenting to an audience gets your stomach in knots, it may help you to remember that you are the expert in the very specific area of work that you intend to present. Science is now so sub-sub-sub specialized, it is extremely likely that nobody else in the room knows much about the work that you are about to present. So feel confident, especially if you have done your homework.

- Practice, practice, practice: nothing gets rid of nerves more efficiently than being totally prepared your presentation. Once you have created a slide deck, practice as much as you can. You don't need to memorize anything, but it does help to have some phrases that you want to use during specific moments of the presentation.

Poster presentations

Poster presentations consist of display boards on which researchers exhibit their work in a condensed format. Scientific conferences will often have concurrent poster sessions with a number of presenters who show their work simultaneously. Posters may be arranged by topic, ensuring that similar posters are placed in close proximity to each other.

If your abstract is accepted, conference organizers will send you instructions for creating your poster, such as guidelines for dimensions, page layout, orientation (portrait or landscape), font requirements or other specifications.

To design your poster, create a layout template in your preferred program (MS PowerPoint in my case). The template should be proportional to the specifications stated in the instructions. This will allow you to have the poster printed to the right size when you send it to the professional printing company of your choice.

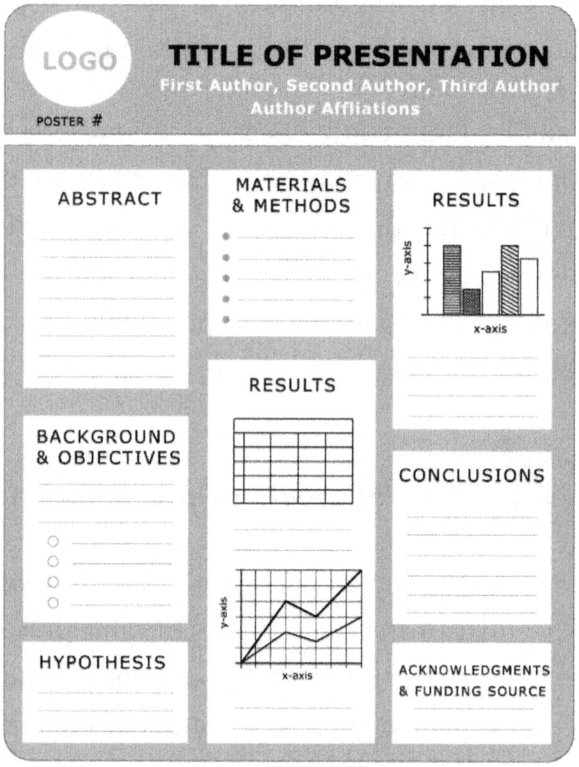

Think of your poster as a concise summary of your work. It should display the main points in easy-to-read bullet points, graphs, charts and other visuals. The font should be large enough to be clearly read from four feet away, and should follow the typical flow of a research paper.

Figure 1: *A poster presentation template*

Conference organizers may ask presenters to display their posters at a designated time, during which presenters are expected to stand next to the poster and answer questions. It can feel a little awkward to stand there waiting for people walk up to you and ask questions or provide comments; however, the idea is to create an environment where conference attendees can visit the posters they are interested in, talk with the presenters and ask questions at a more leisurely pace than what is usually allowed during oral sessions.

Most poster sessions will have at least one hot-topic poster created by a well-known researcher. They generate a ton of interest, and are often surrounded by a crowd of enthusiastic people craning their necks just to get a glimpse or make a comment. If you are not one of these celebrity poster presenters, do not feel intimidated or discouraged. You can still use the conference to elicit the feedback you need.

Tips for great poster presentations

1. **Campaign for your poster**. When you receive the letter of assignment from the conference organizers (which includes information such as your poster number and the date and time when you are expected to display it), be sure to share this information with friends and colleagues. Send actual presentation invitations to any potentially interested individuals and to individuals from whom you want an opinion. This is a good way to promote your work and to get conversations scheduled with people whose input may be helpful to you.

   Don't be shy about promoting your work! When you ask people to attend your presentation, if it is applicable, tell them that you would like their feedback because of their expertise in this area. Remember to reciprocate and view their posters as well.

2. **Practice a walk-through**: When people stop to view your poster, they may ask you to walk them through it. If so, you should provide a brief narrative of the project and point to selected highlights on your poster. You can expect to repeat your presentation over and over again every time someone new stops by.

   Make sure to engage people who have arrived at your poster after you started your walk-through. Try not to ignore people who stand further back while you are talking with someone else. Quickly engage all newcomers with a simple gesture such as making a welcoming hand sign, giving them eye contact, stopping for a moment to say that you will be with them in a few minutes or catching them up to speed with your walk-through presentation.

3. **Create a mini-poster handout**. Conferences can be tiring. Attendees may have traveled from far away to attend, and often have already sat through what feels like a million presentations. It may be that you have the bad luck of being assigned to the poster session that is during the afternoon lull, or the final day when everyone is leaving.

   You can still get good feedback by handing out miniature copies of your poster. This is easy to do if you designed your poster in PowerPoint, although it is possible to do this with almost any program. Print your poster on legal size paper and give it to participants who may not have enough time or energy to closely read your poster during the conference. Make sure to include your contact information on the handout or attach your business card. Encourage people to contact you if they have comments or would like to discuss your results further. This is a good way of networking as well.

4. **Hand out your business card**: Aside from being available to provide additional information to colleagues interested in your investigation, networking with other scientists in your field can lead to collaborations and future employment.

One of the advantages of poster presentations is that they are fairly informal, which gives you the opportunity to talk with colleagues on a one-on-one basis. These interactions can lead to lively exchanges and further networking. Hey, you never know…one of the people you meet this way could end up being your next boss.

5. **Be open-minded**: Some of your viewers may offer negative critiques, provide unsolicited recommendations, or suggest totally different approaches to your research. This is par for the course—the peer-review process at work. And although critiques for submitted papers are given anonymously, poster presentation critiques are given to your face.

Don't be defensive when explaining your work or approach; accept the feedback graciously. Write down all comments as you receive them, getting the commenter's email addresses so that you may follow up on good ideas. The more comments you get, the better.

When you return home from the conference you will have a better perspective, and may not be as sensitive to the comments. Even negative comments can help you (a lot) when it comes time to write the work into a publishable paper. The comments can give you insights into what reviewers may critique when you submit the full paper for publication in a journal. Take it as constructive criticism and understand that in most cases, the critique is not personal. It is intended to improve the research and exchange ideas and expertise.

How conference abstracts are published

Whether you have given an oral or poster presentation, some professional societies publish books of abstracts or proceedings of their conferences. These publications are typically organized by topic and subtopic, and may include a list of presenters and their contact information. Large conferences often publish abstracts on searchable CD-ROMs, flash drives or online, which is very useful when planning which presentations to attend on the days of the conference, and for later reference.

After hosting a conference, professional societies may also publish the conference abstracts in a journal. Some produce a special issue of the journal, or dedicate a part of the journal to the proceedings of their annual conference. This is a good way to see your work published, but be aware that only the abstract portion of your poster or oral presentation will be published in the conference proceedings, not the whole presentation.

Abstracts submitted to a conference are rarely peer-reviewed in depth. For this reason, conference abstracts rarely can be used as citations, and are not counted in the typical NIH-format Biosketch, even when they are published. So although it is a nice thing to put on your resume, published abstracts do very little to advance your academic career.

Points to remember from Chapter 4

- Presenting your work at professional conferences is a great way to obtain feedback about your research from experts in your field who are outside your institution.

- Feedback obtained at a professional conference can help you shape your paper before submitting it for publication.

- Presentations at conferences can be oral or poster presentations. Either way, plan to campaign for your presentation. Invite people from whom you would like feedback to attend your presentation.

- If you are presenting a poster, practice a walk-through and create a mini-poster handout with your contact information as a way to open dialog with fellow researchers.

- Remember that even though there are many benefits to present at professional conferences, most abstracts presented at a conference are not citable, even when they may be published in a proceedings book or journal. The work may be considered preliminary until it is published in a scientific research journal as a complete research paper, not just the abstract.

- Presentation at a professional conference can provide great opportunities for networking, develop collaborations and for exchanging ideas with scientists at other institutions.

Additional Resources

Duarte, Nancy. *Slide:ology: The Art and Science of Creating Great Presentations*, O'Reilly Media, 2008.

Exercise 4: Presenting preliminary work at professional conferences

Write a list of conferences that are important in your field. To make this list:

Ask your mentors about professional conferences that they attend. Look on the websites of journals that you read often. Which of these journals are published by professional societies in your field of research? Do they hold a conference that you would wish to attend? Check their deadlines for abstract submissions. Do you have any data that could be ready for submission to one of these upcoming conferences? Plan ahead and enter those dates in your calendar. Can you get your data ready in time to submit an abstract?

Name of conference, city and date	Abstract submission deadline, website	Draft title of possible abstract to be submitted
Conference of the International Society of Scientists. San Juan, Puerto Rico, February 2018	*June 12, 2017* *www.confer***.org*	*Exposure to toxic element X produces cancer in laboratory rats exposed orally but not subcutaneously*

You may go to www.drluzclaudio.com and download the forms for these exercises, which you will be able to customize to fill in.

Chapter 5: Types of Research Articles

"Either write something worth reading or do something worth writing."
— Benjamin Franklin, one of the founding fathers of the United States, also a scientist, inventor and author.

Now that you have tested the waters with your conference presentations and received constructive feedback for this particular research project, you may be ready to start thinking about moving towards a peer-reviewed submission. Presenting at conferences and other venues, whether it's through an oral or poster presentation, has hopefully given you a good sense of where your project stands, how much more research work you might need to do, what the strongest and weakest points of your data are, and how it compares to the works of others.

While you work through all of this, you should begin to formulate your plans for getting the work ready for publication. To start, let's look at the different types of scientific publications and their function, structure and purpose. You will see that some types of papers require more original data while others require less, but all of them require that the research be carefully scrutinized by other researchers in your field—the essence of the peer-review process.

The original research paper

Also referred to as an *original report, original article*, or *research paper*, these are defined as "a written and published report describing original research." These types of papers publish new data that has not been published elsewhere other than in abstract form at a conference. Research papers are published in academic journals, sometimes called scholarly or peer-reviewed journals.

There are multiple journals for every field or discipline that publish peer-reviewed scholarly research. Some have a broad focus, while others cater to a very specific sub-subspecialty. Wherever you publish your work, publishing key findings of an original research project in a peer-reviewed journal is a fundamental aspect of the scientific endeavor and should be a top priority as you develop and grow in your career.

The process of producing an original research paper involves the following steps:

- Gain a thorough understanding of existing knowledge by reviewing the literature

- Develop a hypothesis-driven study designed to address a gap in knowledge

- Collaborate with other scientists to plan and conduct the research work

- Systematically apply research methods

- Make observations, obtain results, and record data

- Apply analytical methods to decipher and make sense of the data

- Interpret the data analysis in the context of existing knowledge in the field

- Determine whether the original hypothesis was proven or disproven

- Compare and contrast the results obtained with the existing literature

- Obtain input from collaborators and other colleagues

- Explain how these results fill a gap in the current knowledge in the field

- Address any limitations of the study

- Reach insightful conclusions derived from the results

- Receive peer-review and make corrections

- Publish

Through this process, a new finding or a new or unique application is presented to interested readers to add to the existing body of knowledge on a particular topic. The publishing of a research paper is critical for two reasons. First, it expands the knowledge base for the subject area, and second, it shows that the authors have the capacity to create new knowledge in the field of study.

There are several subtypes of original research papers including brief reports, case reports (or case studies), commentaries, review articles, and meta-analyses.

 Publishing original peer-reviewed research is simply the most important thing you will do as a researcher after making your discoveries.

Brief reports

Brief reports are usually short research papers that present results of a small or highly focused study, or a single aspect of a broader study. Brief reports may include reports from pilot studies—these are exploratory studies that are sometimes used to determine the feasibility of a larger investigation.

Journals typically expedite the reviews for brief reports and publish them if the results are likely to be particularly important to the readership. Therefore, brief reports are often a relatively fast way to publish potentially important works.

Consider this Scenario:
A famous Case Report

In 1981, a case report was published describing the clinical presentation of five homosexual men in Los Angeles who all showed with a rare form of pneumonia.

This case report prompted additional case reports from other medical centers in San Francisco and New York. This was an early and important step in identifying AIDS as the similarities between the cases were evidenced and other clinicians became aware of the typical clinical presentation to watch for among their own patient populations.

Case reports and case studies

Case reports and case studies usually describe a novel event or observation. The "case" being reported can be about an individual (a patient or study participant), an organization, a specific study population, or a particular phenomenon or observation.

Case reports can also discuss an example of what happens in a particular situation, and may offer the investigator's suggestions for solutions to the situation. The case can be representative of others, or it can be an outlier or unusual case that presents a novel observation. Caveats should be presented in the paper so that the reader can determine how generalizable the case might be and how it may inform the handling of similar cases or situations that readers may encounter.

Oftentimes, a case report may arise directly from clinical and/or public health practice, as opposed to arising from a planned or systematic research study.

A common example of a case report is the description of a treatment method used on a patient or patients presenting with unusual symptoms in a clinical setting. The reporting of a single case can be viewed as anecdotal, so many authors anchor the writing of the case within the context of a literature review. Thus, a case report may be given as a new example, but backed up by a review of the literature to support the presentation of the case.

A case report can also serve to publicize an emerging illness, prompting other clinicians to keep an eye out for similar cases or to make connections between similarities and differences between cases that can help to detect patterns or highlight potential etiologies and treatments.

Case reports are often descriptive in nature. They usually do not include a comparison or control group, unless it is to compare the case being reported with other similar cases in the literature. The objective of the case report is to recount what happened in a specific instance, as opposed to presenting how a scientific hypothesis was tested and/or data analyzed.

Journals may use different formats when publishing clinical case reports, but usually the article will need to include the following:

- How the case presented in the clinical setting, including any prominent signs and symptoms

- What methods were used to address diagnosis and/or treatment

- The significance of the specific case in the greater clinical context

- Discussion of recommendations for future research or clinical practice

In the current academic climate, clinicians who are associated with an academic medical center are often expected to manage a large number of patients as well as publish scholarly works. These pressures leave little time for designing experimental research.

But, careful observation of patients can sometimes lead to publication-worthy descriptive case reports. Clinicians should be observant and set aside some time to follow through when an opportunity for describing an interesting and potentially important case presents itself that may lead to publication as a case report.

Commentaries

As the name implies, *commentaries* are opportunities for researchers to discuss timely topics in a field, and to comment or present their opinion about a particular issue. Commentaries provide observations on the current state of knowledge surrounding a scientific question, or provide an opinion on the findings of a particular study or a collection of studies.

Shorter than an original research paper, the purpose of a commentary is to provide context for the scientific issue of interest, and to highlight a discussion by a scientist who is considered an expert in that particular field.

Journal editors often invite leaders in their fields—experts—to write commentaries. Some journals accept unsolicited commentaries, but it is usually best to check with the editor-in-chief before submitting this type of paper.

Review articles

Review articles summarize the relevant scientific literature on a specific subject of interest, and may not necessarily contain new scientific information. However, even though review articles generally do not include new data, they can provide a new perspective or insight into a scientific topic and help readers gain an overview of the subject. Writing a review article requires an especially thorough understanding of the topic to be discussed.

Similar to commentaries, many journals publish review articles by invitation only. In those cases, the editor-in-chief may ask a well-known expert to submit a review on a topic that is of particular interest to its readers. If you feel that you are an expert in a particular field, you may consider proposing a review article to an editor.

> ### *Consider this scenario: meta-analysis*
>
> A statistician finds that there are 50 published research papers reporting on the effects of Drug X on kidney function. Of these, only 25 studies measured a particular marker to assess kidney function. Each one of these studies published results based on research using 1,000 patients. Given that the methods used in these 25 studies were comparable, the statistician is able to reanalyze the data corresponding to 25,000 patients, thus improving the confidence intervals of the results. The results of the meta-analysis will be more generalizable than the results of the original studies taken individually, and would therefore provide a better estimation of the effects of Drug X.

A well-written review article includes a detailed description of the methodology used to identify the relevant literature that will be included in the review. Often referred to as a *systematic review*, this type of article includes a methodology for selecting, reviewing and extracting the articles included in the review. As part of the description of these methods, the article may cite the database used to obtain the articles (such as Pubmed, SciELO, etc.), the search terms used, the inclusion and exclusion criteria, any method used for systematic review and extraction of information from the papers, dates of the literature search, methods for analysis and any other methods or criteria applied.

The application of this kind of systematic methodology ensures that a fair and balanced review of the scientific literature is conducted, and it minimizes the potential for bias when selecting which studies to include in the review article.

Meta-analyses

The meta-analysis is a study in which data from other articles is pooled and re-analyzed to yield a new, more comprehensive set of data on which to base conclusions. Meta-analyses are very useful in instances where no single research group has been able to collect enough study participants to make conclusive observations of a particular phenomenon. For example, a biostatistician may decide to conduct a meta-analysis to pool data from eight separate controlled clinical trials of a new experimental drug that is being tested for the treatment of a relatively rare disease. The meta-analysis would provide greater statistical power than each individual clinical trial, because the number of patients in the meta-analysis would be much greater than the number of patients in each individual clinical trial.

One key for being able to complete a successful meta-analysis is to be able to find a reasonable number of studies that have used very similar methods on comparable subjects. This is not always possible, but worth exploring.

Points to remember from Chapter 5

- You should aim to write an original research paper.

- You can get ideas for papers by reading other papers in your field. Observe how they are structured, the phrases and terms used, and the way the data is illustrated. Use papers that you cite often, or papers that are in a similar area as your research as inspiration for your own papers.

- Brief reports, case studies and commentaries are important venues for publication.

- Case studies (or case reports) are particularly good opportunities for clinicians to publish in the scientific literature.

- Review articles are usually written by high-level experts. Oftentimes, journal editors request review articles from well-known experts.

- Meta-analyses are studies in which the data from several different studies are pooled in order to increase the power of the observations.

Additional Resources

Booth, Wayne C., Colomb, Gregory G., and Williams, Joseph M. *The Craft of Research,* Third Edition. University of Chicago Press, 2009.

Exercise 5a: Getting ideas for papers

Write ideas for two papers based on your research or clinical practice. If no clear ideas jump to mind, ask yourself these questions: Have I had any interesting clinical cases that may be suitable for a case report? Do I have enough expertise and information to write a review or a commentary? What kinds of articles would I be able to write right now with the data I already have? Do I have enough data for an original research paper? What is the current status of that data? Is it gathered? Is it being analyzed? Have figures or tables been created?

An example of this step is provided below. Fill in your information in the blanks.

Topic, theme or main idea of potential paper	Type of article (original research paper, review, commentary, case report, etc.)	Status of data
Results from study on educational intervention on asthma in children	*Original research paper*	*Data collection complete. Analysis on full database being completed. Presented pilot data. Need final graphs.*

You may go to www.drluzclaudio.com and download the forms for the following exercises, which you will be able to customize to fill in.

Exercise 5b: *Getting even more ideas for papers*

Take a look at articles that you have read recently. What types of articles are they? Do you see a commentary or a review among them? Do you sometimes think, "I could have written this!" Make a list of three articles of different types that you have recently read. Include a comment noting whether you have the expertise and data to write a similar article. What would be different about your article that would expand on what these articles have already done? Get inspired!

Article citation	Type of article	Comment
Doe J. et al., Patient with rare disease: Case report and review of literature. Am. J Cases	*Case report*	*I have a similar case with a different outcome. Should publish commentary on this one. Check with collaborator.*

STOP!

Throughout the remaining text, you will see several suggestions for repurposing existing material. Before you edit and reuse any existing content, make sure that YOU were the author of that work and that it has not been published elsewhere. If one of your coauthors wrote the original materials that you intend to repurpose, ask for their permission and make sure that they did not publish it previously. In spite of these caveats, you will be surprised how much other writing you may have already completed that would kick start you into publishing your new paper. Once you have found appropriate materials to repurpose, make sure to thoroughly adapt it specifically for the paper that you are now writing. It can become quite obvious if you don't.

Chapter 6: Writing the Outline

"If you don't know where you are going you might wind up someplace else."

– Lawrence Peter "Yogi" Berra, American baseball player and coach

After you have decided what set of data (or more accurately, what data figures) you will be including in your paper, you will need to create a detailed plan of how you will structure your paper—an outline.

The outline serves as a roadmap that points you toward your desired destination. It is the tool that you will use to organize your information. It is the skeleton on which the meat of your paper will be attached. It is the scaffold on which you hand your ideas. It is... We can go on with analogies, but it will never be a hyperbole. The outline is the most important, yet invisible, part of writing a research paper. Just believe me, it is very important.

When first writing the outline, you should closely follow the main sections of the paper. As you may know, most scientific papers follow this general format:

- **Title page**
- **Abstract**
- **Introduction**
- **Materials and methods**
- **Results with tables and figures**
- **Discussion and Conclusions**
- **References**

Within each of these main headings, you should include subsections that expand each topic and that help organize the information under each of the main headings. The headings and subheadings will serve you as prompts to extract your ideas in an organized, direct and logical way.

As you write, your goal should be to present each premise and then provide increasing detail of the evidence that you found to support that premise. This mode of writing is often described as *deductive writing*. More information about how to write each section will be given in Chapter 9. But for now, for the purpose of writing a solid outline, keep in mind to use deductive writing by being direct in your use of headings and subheadings.

For the most part, the outline instructions in this chapter can be applied to most original research papers submitted to most journals in the biomedical sciences. You can modify and adapt these guidelines as you see fit for your own research. You can make any adaptations based on your experience, the format of journals that you usually read and input from mentors and colleagues.

I don't think that there is an outline template that will fit all research papers, but the instructions presented in this chapter will fit most papers for most journals.

 Why you need an outline

- An outline will help you to see the whole picture at a glance, making it easier to determine what should stay in the paper and what might be information better suited for another paper.

- An outline will help you divide the work into doable chunks. Seeing it in outline format makes writing the paper an achievable goal.

- An outline will help you to organize materials and sources, and can be helpful when involving collaborators for writing certain sections if necessary.

Instructions for writing an outline for an original research paper

I.   **TITLE AND ABSTRACT – *THE LABEL and SUMMARY***

The title and abstract are the only parts of your paper that will appear in most search engines and literature databases. For this reason, the title and abstract are extremely important. Think about the title and abstract as invitations for potential readers who will use it to decide whether they want to download and read the rest of your paper.

a. **Title**: Statement that describes the content of the paper. Elements that can be included in the title are:

i. The type of study that was conducted (a randomized trial, a case-control study, an *in vitro* study, a community-based intervention, etc.),

ii. The kind of subjects on which your research protocol was conducted (Sprague-Dawley rats, endothelial cell cultures, high school children, wild common marmosets, etc.),

iii. The main conclusion of the study (socioeconomic status is associated with obesity rates, exposure to lead lowers neurotransmission in neurons),

iv. Where the study was conducted (New York City, Amazonian rainforest, Antarctic).

The title should include enough detail for the reader to be able to determine the content of the paper while doing so with an economy of words. Most journals have a word or character limit for how long a title can be and you must follow that guideline which is usually found in the instructions for authors.

b. **Abstract**: A self-contained summary of the full contents of the paper. It should include a brief statement of the background, a summary of the study design and methods used, the main results and conclusions. It can include some of the specific results found in the study. For example, an epidemiological study may include the numerical results of disease prevalence rates. Structured abstracts include subtitles for the different sections while unstructured abstracts can be more free-flowing. The abstract should not include any figures or references and it should be self-contained, meaning that all of the most important information about the study should be included within the abstract. Reading the abstract should give a very good and complete idea of what the paper is about, the approach that was taken and the most important results and conclusions.

II. INTRODUCTION — *THE WHY*

The introduction explains why you conducted the study. It should provide details as to why this topic is important and why you approached this particular scientific question, problem or the knowledge gap that your paper intends to fill. You should justify the existence of your paper. Why should this work matter to the reader?

a. **Background**: Include the scientific background and explanation of the rationale of why this study was conducted. State its significance and why it is important. The background should set the stage for the rest of the paper. It should contain most of the information that readers should know beforehand in order to understand the rest of the paper.

b. **Objectives**: Explain the hypothesis or specific objectives that guided the study. Lead the reader to understand the approach that you took to address the issue presented in the background statements.

III. MATERIALS AND METHODS – *THE HOW*

The materials and methods are the recipe detailing how the study was conducted. You need to provide enough information in this section to allow a competent researcher in your field to replicate your results if they had access to the same study subjects. You should explain HOW you did the research, including how the study was designed, subjects selected, experiments conducted, data analyzed, etc.

a. **Study design**: Describe in detail the design concepts that were applied. For example, in the case of a randomized controlled clinical trial, the study design section would detail how the study population was assigned to the different treatment groups such as using parallel, factorial, and allocation ratios for the study population.

b. **Participants/subjects**: Describe the study population in detail. This could be human subjects, laboratory animals, cell cultures, etc. For example, if your subject is a cell-line, give details of its source or how it was created. If you used laboratory animals, provide the name and location of the supplier. If you used human subjects, describe how they were selected.

c. **Study settings**: Provide information about the settings and locations where the data was collected, if relevant. This is particularly important in population-based studies.

d. **Interventions/experiments**: Make sure to include all the details about how the intervention, experiments, observations, or any action that you took to conduct the study. Explain how your work was conducted, and provide enough detail to allow other scientists to replicate your study (but not so much detail as to be redundant or state the obvious).

e. **Outcome measures**: Explain all primary and secondary outcome measures and how they were assessed. For example, if you used a particular method or tool (such as a previously-validated questionnaire, a type of chemical assay, or a test method for child development), describe how the outcomes were measured using the selected tool.

f. **Sample size**: Give the calculations that led to the determination of the final sample size. For many kinds of studies, you must provide the sample size calculations. For instance, for a clinical trial in which a number of subjects were recruited to test a new drug.

You can also include here how many times (repeats) you conducted the experiments. This applies especially to studies that require you to conduct the same experiment multiple times, such as experiments on cell cultures.

g. **Interim analysis and stopping guidelines (for clinical trials)**: Sometimes during clinical trials, it may become necessary to conduct some analyses prior to the completion of the study. For example, if a potential danger that may affect study participants is found during interim analyses, the clinical trial may be stopped. Reasons for stopping the trial or for stopping the participation of some subjects in the study should be included.

h. **Randomization and blinding**: If your research involved assigning subjects to different experimental groups, provide details of the method for random selection or allocation of participants into the different trial groups. You should also provide information on how the randomization protocol was implemented, and whether blinding was part of the study design. This may not apply to all types of studies, but it can be a useful way to ensure validity or impartiality of the results of many study types.

i. **Analytical methods**: Write a clear description of the methods used to assess the results, especially any statistical analysis methods and other analyses such as adjusted analyses. Include any statistical software packages, any tests used to assess significance and any other analyses applied to the experimental data.

IV. RESULTS - *THE WHAT*

The results section is where you will list the observations and findings that stemmed from conducting your study. This is where you will recount what happened after you conducted your experiments and where you will guide the reader through the evidence that you obtained, as illustrated in your figures and tables.

a. **Baseline data**: Provide here any information that helps describe the study subjects prior to when the experimental actions where implemented. Providing this information helps the reader understand the characteristics of the subjects that you studied in your research. For example, in a clinical trial, you may provide a table showing the baseline demographic data and other characteristics of the study populations that may be important as background for understanding the population studied.

b. **Participant flow chart:** For several types of studies, such as clinical trials and other types of human subjects studies, there are guidelines for reporting on study participants. In the CONSORT statement (described later in this chapter) you must include an explanation of the numbers of participants who received the intended treatments for each experimental or control group.

   To do this, you may include explanations of participants who were lost from the study or otherwise excluded, and the reasons for their exclusion. This is particularly useful when writing papers that involved the recruitment of human subjects from a larger pool of potential participants. This type of information can be given as a flow diagram as part of the paper, or as supplementary information when the journal allows for this additional information to be included online.

c. **Numbers and outcomes**: For each group, provide the final numbers (denominator) on which outcome measures were estimated for each experimental or control group. Include a measure of precision of the outcome results (such as confidence intervals or range). Include summary data within the text and more detailed data in the tables and figures.

d. **Data analyses**: Include results of any additional analysis such as results from a subgroup analysis or an adjusted analysis. Data numbers that are the result of additional analyses (not directly resulting from the experiments) should be clearly shown as ancillary analyses that were derived from the experimental data.

e. **Harms**: Include all important harms experienced by the participants for any unintended effects in each group (for clinical trials).

V. DISCUSSION – *THE SO WHAT*

The purpose of the discussion section is to give you the opportunity to put your results into context, compare them to results obtained by others and provide explanations for your findings. Generally, the discussion section should be organized following the same general flow of the results section. Thus, each of the results should be discussed in this section in the same order that they were presented in the results section. The items that should be included in the discussion section are:

f. **Interpretation**: Provide contextual explanations based on the results of the study and all relevant evidence to substantiate any conclusions. Compare and contrast the results that you obtained with results from other studies.

g. **Limitations**: State any sources of potential bias, imprecision in the measures, or any other issues that could limit the interpretation of results. This would include, for example, a low number of participants, inconsistency between repeated experiments, unreliability of a measurement or any other caveats that could potentially impede the accuracy of the results.

h. **Generalizability**: Provide information on how broadly the results apply to other situations, populations, types of subjects or variants. Explain how the results may be applied or may be valid for other studies, or how it may illuminate conduct of similar experiments in other settings.

i. **Conclusions**: Provide some final takeaway thoughts based on the data obtained. Ensure that your conclusions are based on the data contained in the paper and the context that is provided in the discussion section. The evidence for the conclusions should be logically derived from the information given in the previous sections of the paper.

These instructions for creating an outline for a research paper can be adapted and applied to almost any kind of research study that you may want to prepare for publication. The most important thing to learn about creating an outline is that each section of your paper should be very focused and circumscribed to the specific topic at hand. The outline should follow a logical flow that will be dictated by the outcomes of your research results. After doing this a few times, I guarantee that it will become increasingly easy and extremely useful.

Spend time creating a solid outline. It will be time well spent.

Standardized guidelines and checklists

To ensure scientific transparency, study reproducibility, and clarity of writing, some expert groups have created standardized checklists that detail the types of information that should be included in scientific articles in their fields. Some journals require the use of these guidelines for certain types of studies, such as randomized controlled trials and epidemiological studies.

Even if your journal of choice does not require the use of these checklists or guidelines, some may be helpful in preparing your outline, writing your manuscript, and ensuring that all of the important and relevant information is included in your draft. Descriptions of two such checklists or guidelines are included below.

The CONSORT statement

The Consolidated Standards for Reporting Trials (CONSORT) is a 22-item checklist used to improve the clarity of articles based on randomized controlled trials. It also recommends the use of a flow diagram that tracks participants through the different stages of the clinical trial, so readers can evaluate exactly how the participants were included/excluded in the analysis. I will talk more about this in Chapter 9. The CONSORT checklist has been extended for use with study designs beyond the standard randomized controlled trials, including cluster trials, equivalence trials, trials of herbal interventions, and trials of non-pharmacological treatments.

If your paper is a randomized controlled trial or a population study in which population groups are selected according to applied criteria, you may consider using this checklist and including the flow diagram in your paper. More information about the CONSORT Statement can be found here: ***http://www.consort-statement.org/***

The STROBE guidelines

The STROBE (Strengthening the Reporting of Observational studies in Epidemiology) guidelines are a set of checklists and supporting documentation for various types of observational epidemiological studies. The STROBE is an international collaborative initiative of statisticians, researchers, epidemiologists and other experts in epidemiological methods that have teamed up with journal editors to provide a checklist that can guide the publication of observational studies in epidemiology. On their website, there are several useful checklists for different kinds of studies such as cross-sectional studies, case-control studies, and cohort studies. There is a growing number of biomedical journals that have endorsed (but not necessarily required) the STROBE guidelines.

Some other examples of checklists include:

MOOSE: Meta-Analysis of Observational Studies in Epidemiology

QUORUM: Quality of Reporting of Meta-Analyses

REMARK: Reporting Recommendations for Tumor Marker Prognostic Studies

STARD: Standards for Reporting of Diagnostic Accuracy

TREND: Transparent Reporting of Evaluations with Nonrandomized Designs

More information about the STROBE guidelines can be found at: ***http://www.strobe-statement.org/***

Professional societies have put together guidelines that can serve as outlines for certain types of publications, such as clinical trials. Check with the journal's __Instructions for Authors__ to determine if any specific guidelines apply to your paper.

Organizing your materials based on your outline

Your outline should serve as your framework for organizing your ideas and materials for the paper. It is the skeleton that you will flesh-out when you write. As such, it is a useful tool for organizing your source material.

To use the outline most effectively, I recommend creating folders (electronic or paper) labeled for each of the outline headings. Use whatever method works best for your style. For example, I print the reference research articles that I will use and put them in the appropriate folder or subfolder. This makes it easier for me to envision the entire work, and allows me to write notes on reference materials and on other supporting or source documents.

To organize your documents, you can use file folders, binders with dividers, upright or flat document boxes, or you can simply keep them as folders, files and subfiles in your computer. Use the method that best fits your style. For the purpose of simplicity, I will use the word "folder" for either paper or electronic filing systems.

Organizing your materials is relatively easy once you have a solid outline. Follow these general steps and you will not fail:

1. Create a main folder for each of the sections of your paper: *introduction, materials and methods, results,* and *discussion.*

2. Within each of these folders, create subfolders or divisions for each of the topics in each section, corresponding to your outline.

3. Focus first on the folder labeled "**Results**". This is going to be the heart of your paper. Within this folder, file your final data, tables, charts, graphs and any other figures that you will use in your paper to illustrate your data. Within this folder, organize your figures in a logical order or flow. The data can be organized starting with general findings and ending with specific or detailed findings. This way, the data builds upon itself and follows a logical trajectory, which will make it easier for you to write about.

4. Create your **Introduction** folder to include all reference literature that provides background for the topic of your paper. These should include articles that give information about the importance of the research question, the state of knowledge at the moment, the scope or magnitude of the issue to be investigated, how has it been investigated in the past, current hypotheses, previous theorems, and other papers that will give the reader a good perspective on your reasons for pursuing this investigation. Within the folder, organize the literature following your outlined subtopics.

5. In your **Materials and Methods** folder, file information that will help you describe the resources, supplies, ingredients, populations, tools, any equipment you used to conduct the studies and how you used them. For some of your more specialized materials, you may need to include the manufacturer's or supplier's name and location. You may also include previous papers that reference a particular technique you used in your study.

6. In your **Discussion** folder, file reference literature that has previously addressed the central issue that you present in your paper. You may include papers that have pursued similar investigations, have obtained similar or opposite results on the same research question or have previously addressed the issue in different ways. Include any papers that are comparable to yours in topic and/or approach to the research question. Follow your outline.

There you have it. A nice, perfectly organized filing system that will stimulate you to write and keep you on track and focused. It will also help you keep everything you need for writing conveniently at hand. This way, you will be able to write without having to stop to search for additional information or for references.

Get into the habit of outlining and creating folders and subfolders that follow your outline. As you start having several outlines for research publications going at once, you will also be able to cross-reference some of the materials by keeping them in the outline system. This may be the most important step in this book. Even though you may not have written a single word of your paper (except the title) you are already halfway there if you have accomplished a solid outline and organized your materials based on it.

Points to remember from Chapter 6

- It is essential that you write an outline, even if you think that you have a good vision about how to structure your paper, and even if you have a lot of writing experience.

- An outline should follow the general sections of a research paper as main headings.

- The outline serves several important functions:

  - ➢ A tool for organizing your materials. You can use the outline to create files in which to organize the literature to be cited, the figures and tables and any other source material that may be needed as you focus on writing the paper.

  - ➢ A roadmap to guide your writing. The outline lets you see the flow of ideas to be incorporated into the paper and lets you see how each of the parts of the paper will relate to each other. With an outline you will be able to see the beginning, middle and end of your paper.

  - ➢ Stimulation for collaborating with colleagues. You can designate sections to be written by others and divide the work into doable pieces for your own writing or to delegate to others.

  - ➢ A template that helps you avoid confronting a blank page and alleviates writer's block.

- A few professional associations have created guidelines to aide in the standardization of research reporting. One example is The Consolidated Standards for Reporting Trials (CONSORT) statement, which includes a checklist for reporting clinical trials.

Resources

STROBE -Strengthening the Reporting of Observational studies in Epidemiology
http://www.strobe-statement.org

CONSORT - The Consolidated Standards for Reporting Trials
http://www.consort-statement.org

Anatomy of a research paper

Anatomy Of A Research Paper

I.   **TITLE PAGE**: The title is a *LABEL*. It is a descriptive statement of exactly what is in the paper. In addition to the title, the title page will have all identifying information such as names of authors and affiliations. Many journals want this information on a separate page that can be separated from the rest of the paper in order to make the review process blind.

II.   **ABSTRACT**: This is the *SUMMARY* of the full paper in a very short, abbreviated format. The abstract should be self-contained. It should not require the reader to seek out other information in order to get a good understanding of the full paper. For example, the abstract should not include citations or refer to figures or tables in the paper.

III.   **INTRODUCTION**: The introduction explains *WHY* the work was done. This is the background information that led you to do this research. You should present the scientific problem and state the scientific information that led you to conduct this research question.

IV.   **MATERIALS AND METHODS**: This section describes *HOW* the work was done. In this section, you need to provide detailed information about how you conducted the research project.

V.   **RESULTS**: This is the *WHAT* of the study. What was observed? What was found? What was the output of your project? Refer to tables and figures in this section.

VI.   **DISCUSSION**: In this section, you will explain the *SO WHAT* of your work. Here you will discuss what the results mean. How do the results compare to others in the literature? This is where you make sense of the results obtained.

VII.   **CONCLUSIONS**: Briefly summarize the main findings of the paper and their significance. Some journals require the conclusions to be a separate section, while most require that is be included in the discussion section.

You may want to cut and paste this page onto your work area for easy reference

This page left blank so you may cut page 79 out of the book, if desired.

Exercise 6a: Template for outline

To create a strong and useful outline that will serve you well through the process of writing your paper, use the template below to organize your thoughts and materials. Included are questions that will prompt your writing in a logical flow. I suggest that you answer the questions in the outline template given below in "lay language"—language that can be understood by people outside your field. You may want to dictate or speak some of these sections out loud, which tends to improve the clarity and directness of the statements. This will help you to practice writing with clarity.

Note that this template applies specifically to the format most commonly used for original research papers. However, other types of papers can be organized in a similar format.

EXAMPLE (For illustration purposes only):

I.   **TITLE:** Association between socioeconomic factors and asthma rates in children: A population-based epidemiologic study using government data

II.   **INTRODUCTION**: The introduction explains *WHY* the work was done. This is the background information that led you to do this research. You should present the scientific problem and state the scientific information that led you to conduct this research question.

1. **Why is this topic important?**
   Asthma is the most common respiratory disease in the US. Close to 4 million children are affected.

2. **What is known about the topic? What are some important facts?**
   Asthma is very common among minority communities. It is highly prevalent in children, being one of the main causes of absenteeism. Asthma can be caused or aggravated by environmental exposures, lack of follow-up, and poor access to care. These factors may be more prevalent in minority communities.

3. **What are some gaps in the current knowledge about this topic?**
   It is not known how the prevalence of asthma varies between populations of different socioeconomic status and how these socioeconomic factors may affect the rates and severity of the disease.

4. **Why did you conduct this work? What is the rationale?**
   Asthma affects many people and it is increasing in prevalence around the world. It is possible that understanding socioeconomic factors that affect asthma rates and severity could help in understanding health disparities.

5. State your hypothesis.

Minority and low-income communities in Major City have higher prevalence of the socioeconomic and environmental factors that we think may cause or trigger asthma. We hypothesize that asthma prevalence rates will be higher among minority communities as a direct consequence of exposure to these factors.

6. What are the specific objectives of the work? How were the objectives approached?

The primary objective is to determine asthma prevalence rates in all communities in New York City. The secondary objectives were to determine the relationship between asthma prevalence rates and socioeconomic factors including household income, race, ethnicity, primary language, nativity, health insurance and access to preventive care.

III.   **MATERIALS AND METHODS**: This section answers the question of *HOW* the work was done. In this section, you need to provide detailed information about how you conducted the research project.

1. Setting and study design.
Description of the database obtained from the Department of Health

2. Describe the subjects of the research such as human population, cells, tissues or animals used. Source of particular or unique materials and resources.
Residents of Major City who reported to city hospitals with a diagnosis of asthma. Database created by the Department of Health._(Refer to the database description documents).

    a. **State that the research was reviewed and approved by your Institutional Review Board (IRB) or Institutional Animal Care and Use Committee (IACUC) regarding the use of subjects of the research (humans or laboratory animals).**

3. State the sampling methods. Criteria for inclusion/exclusion.
Residential zip code within the three boroughs. Primary diagnosis of asthma in last 12 months. Children and adults based on CDC age groups.

4. Describe any experimental procedures conducted on the subjects of the research.
Extracted data through queries of the database including: ICD-10 code, age, residence.

5. **Variables, outcomes measured, tools, definitions, predictors, potential confounders, effect modifiers, procedures, description of databases or other data sources:**

   Queried diagnosis, severity, household income, place of birth, preferred language.

6. **Methods for measuring and observing the results. Refer to methods from other studies and their sources if needed.**

   Refer to our previous study from 2008.

7. **Data analysis methods, statistical analysis procedures, specialized data visualization tools.**

   Used statistical software program X for data analysis, chi-squared statistic for categorical variables and the Wald test for continuous variables corrected for study design with svy-procedures. Adjusted odds ratios with logistic regression procedure in statistical software program X. Significance at $p < .5$. Arc GIS for maps.

IV. **RESULTS**: This is the **WHAT** of the study. What was observed? What was found? What was the output of your project? Refer to tables and figures.

   1. **Descriptive data.**

      Table of demographics showing how the sample compared to the overall population.

   2. **Results of outcomes and observations.**

      The rates of asthma were higher among Latinos, then African Americans, then other races. Income was a determining factor in asthma rates. Show tables with asthma prevalence rate per group.

   3. **Main results, unadjusted data outcomes.**

      Graph of asthma prevalence rates by group.
      Table of rates of asthma by zip code showing clusters.

   4. **Other analyses on subgroups or interactions, sensitivity analyses, additional comparisons and statistical tests.**

      Table of independent effects by demographic characteristic adjusted by age and gender.

V. **DISCUSSION**. In this section, you will explain the **SO WHAT** of your work. Here you try to describe what the results mean. How they compare to others in the literature. This is where you make sense of the data.

1. **How do key results compare to other studies?**

   Compare with national trends as published by Dr. X (list main papers that show comparable results). Compare and contrast results from National statistics from CDC, other cities (compare to studies in California, Boston, etc.), other studies in Major City.

2. **Limitations.**

   Potential enrollment bias, misclassification of racial categories, errors in geographical boundaries for coding zip codes.

3. **Interpretation.**

   Consistent with studies done by Dr. X and Dr. Y (main authors who have done comparable studies). Inconsistent with studies done by Dr. Z (studies that may be in disagreement with your results).

4. **Generalizability.**

   Our large sample size reduced measurement error. Results can be applied to other urban cities with similar populations.

5. **Conclusions and recommendations.**

   There are clear disparities in asthma rates among urban populations. These disparities are tightly correlated to low income, but not to race/ethnicity. Clustering of asthma rates my indicate areas where additional intervention resources should be allocated.

Exercise 6b: Template for outline

I.   **TITLE:**

_____

_____

_____

_____

II.   **INTRODUCTION**: The introduction explains *WHY* the work was done. This is the background information that led you to do this research. You should present the scientific problem and state the scientific information that led you to conduct this research question.

    1. **Why is this topic important?**

_____

_____

_____

_____

    2. **What is known about the topic? What are some important facts?**

_____

_____

_____

_____

    3. **What are some gaps in the current knowledge about this topic?**

_____

_____

_____

_____

_____

4. Why did you conduct this work? What is the rationale?

_____

_____

_____

_____

_____

_____

5. State your hypothesis.

_____

_____

_____

_____

_____

6. What are the specific objectives of the work?

_____

_____

_____

_____

_____

_____

III. MATERIALS AND METHODS: This section answers the question of **_HOW_** the work was done. In this section, you need to provide detailed information about how you conducted the research project.

1. Setting and study design.

_____

_____

a. State that the research was reviewed and approved by your Institutional Review Board (IRB) or Institutional Animal Care and Use Committee (IACUC) regarding the use of subjects of the research (humans or laboratory animals).

_____

_____

_____

_____

2. Describe the subjects of the research such as human population, cells, tissues or animals used. Source of particular or unique materials and resources.

_____

_____

_____

_____

_____

3. State the sampling methods. Criteria for inclusion/exclusion.

_____

_____

_____

_____

4. Describe any experimental procedures conducted on the subjects of the research.

_____

_____

_____

_____

_____

5. Variables, outcomes measured, tools, definitions, predictors, potential confounders, effect modifiers, procedures, description of databases or other data sources.

_____

_____

_____

_____

6. Methods for measuring and observing the results. Refer to methods from other studies and their sources if needed.

_____

_____

_____

_____

7. Data analysis methods, statistical analysis procedures, specialized data visualization tools.

_____

_____

_____

_____

IV.   **RESULTS**: This is the *WHAT* of the study. What was observed? What was found? What was the output of your project? Refer to tables and figures.

1. **Descriptive data.**

_____

_____

_____

_____

2. **Results of outcomes and observations.**

_____

_____

3. **Main results, unadjusted data outcomes.**

_____

_____

_____

_____

4. **Other analyses on subgroups or interactions, sensitivity analyses, additional comparisons and statistical tests.**

_____

_____

_____

_____

V. **DISCUSSION**: In this section, you will explain the *SO WHAT* of your work. Here you try to describe what the results mean. How they compare to others in the literature. This is where you make sense of the data.

1. **How do key results compare to other studies?**

_____

_____

_____

_____

2. **Limitations.**

_____

_____

_____

_____

3. **Interpretation.**

_____

_____

_____

_____

4. **Generalizability.**

_____

_____

_____

_____

5. **Conclusions and recommendations.**

_____

_____

_____

_____

You may go to www.drluzclaudio.com and download the forms for the following exercises, which you will be able to customize to fill in.

Chapter 7: Choosing a Journal

"It is our choices… that show what we truly are, far more than our abilities."

– J.K. Rowling, British author

 Selecting the right journal for your paper is a key decision that can determine whether your paper gets published. It can be a daunting task, given the myriad of scientific journals available and the fact that your work may be related to a number of them. As of today, there were 5,635 journals indexed in Medline, the publisher of PubMed.

Luckily, there are systematic and effective ways to search, sort, and examine those journals in order to choose one that will consider publishing your paper. There are some different approaches to examining which journals to consider. Below I detail three of these approaches.

Follow the clues

Using the "follow the clues" approach requires you to be observant of the literature that has been published in your field. To use this approach, follow these clues:

1. Notice which journals published the articles that you have collected as background information for your paper. Have many of them been published in the same journal? If so, this may be a journal you may want to consider for your own publication.

2. Do you or your mentor have a subscription to a journal that you read often? If so, this may be one journal you might want to consider.

3. Have you presented an abstract of the work that you intend to publish at a conference of a professional society that also publishes a journal? This journal may target the audience that would be most interested in your work.

4. Who would be most interested in your research: clinicians, public health practitioners, academic researchers, policy makers? You want to reach a particular audience with your paper. Consider the potential readership for whom the information would be most useful. Is there a journal that caters to this particular audience?

Advantages to this approach: It best ensures that people who are most interested in your topic will see your paper.

Disadvantages: You will end up preaching to the choir of people who have the same or similar approaches to your research question.

Walk to the library

"Seriously?" you ask. Yes, seriously. A good medical library is not only a quiet place to study and take a nap. It also employs a librarian—a person with a wealth of information that could be a great help to you in your quest to finding a home for your research paper. For this approach, follow these steps:

1. Using your working title, identify the specific topic of your article.

2. Go to your medical library and talk to the librarian. Ask for suggestions of relevant journals based on your working title.

3. Peruse the latest issues of several journals related to your topic. Examine the tables of contents of at least the latest three issues of the journal to assess if they have recently published articles of similar scope, theme and level of impact as you intend your paper to be based on your results and outline.

4. Photocopy the Instructions for Authors, contact information, and other relevant information from the two or three journals that best fit your paper.

Advantages of this approach: Requires you to leave your desk (which may be a good thing once in a while). A librarian can bring you another perspective on the potential outlets for your paper.

Disadvantages: Some libraries no longer carry print versions of many journals, and many journals are only published online, so if you only look in the stacks you will miss some potentially good journals. To avoid this pitfall, ask your librarian for assistance.

Let your fingers do the walking

It is such a great advantage that now almost all journals have very comprehensive websites that include all relevant information that is needed for submitting a research paper for their consideration. Many peer reviewed journals are now managed under big publishing companies that handle all submissions and publications under one large website umbrella. Elsevier, the British Medical Journal (BMJ), Springer, and Oxford are some of the large publishers that come to mind.

Whether the journal that you select to approach for publishing your paper is managed as part of one of these large publishing companies or is published through a smaller operation, you will need to make a judgment call as to which journal is right for your paper. Finding the right journal for your paper is quite a job in itself.

The first step is to find the journals that publish in your research discipline. One good way to do so is by using the National Library of Medicine catalog of journals referenced in the National Center for Biotechnology Information (NCBI). Searching this database will give you a list of journals that publish papers in the same area defined by your keywords.

Make sure to bookmark the link below in your browser. This is one of the most useful tools that you will have for accessing journal information online:

 To search for a journal (not an individual article) in PubMed, go to: http://www.ncbi.nlm.nih.gov/entrez/query.fcgi?db=Journals

Steps for using PubMed to search for the right journal for your paper

1. Go to the URL listed above. Using this portal, you can search journals by entering a word or phrase that best fits your topic. PubMed will give you a list of journals that contain that word or phrase in their titles or as part of their main keywords. When searching using this system, you will need to conduct more than one search in order to refine your lists.

For example, a search for the word *cancer* yields 595 journals, while searching for the words *breast cancer* yields 16. (Note that the phrase should be in quotation marks so that the whole phrase is searched, not just the individual words). For example, following is a screen capture showing five of the journals that appear when searching for the term *"breast cancer"* which yielded a total of 12 journals (sorted in alphabetical order).

Consider also that your work may fit in different topics depending on what aspect you want to emphasize in your paper. You can refine your search by being more specific in your search terms or by using some of the filters in the search engine such as limiting your search to a particular language or country of publication.

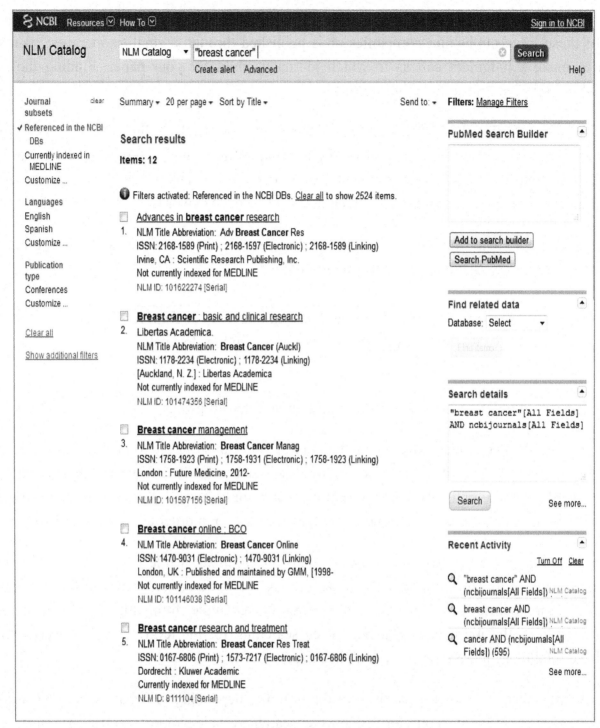

Figure 1: Example of a Pubmed Search

2. For most journals, you can click on the name or the NLM ID link to go directly to the home page of the journal. If you have access to a medical library that has unlimited subscriptions to many journals, then you most likely will have free access to the journal contents. Look for the Instructions for Authors, usually located on the *About this Journal* page. These pages are the main sources of information that you can use to make a decision as to which journal to pursue.

For instance, in the previous example, you could eliminate some journals and consider only those that are most relevant. Looking through the list, you notice that you can eliminate some journals based on the title. If your research is focused on the treatment of breast cancer in the clinical setting, then journals #4 or #5 (Figure 1) may be a good fit. On the other hand, if your work is more related to breast cancer management, you might want to consider journal #3. The idea here is to narrow down your search using appropriate terms for the topic of your paper.

Also consider that your work may be suited for different journals depending on the aspect of the paper that you consider most important. For example, if you conducted your work on breast cancer using cell culture methods, there may be cell biology journals that would publish your work rather than a journal solely focused on breast cancer.

Likewise, if your work on breast cancer had to do with genes that predict severity of disease, perhaps a journal on genetics would be appropriate. If your approach is community based, then a search using those appropriate terms would yield yet another set of journals for you to consider. So, you may think of choosing journals based on different aspects of your paper, not just the disease being addressed or your disciplinary branch of the sciences.

Advantages of this approach: You will have several possibilities in a matter of minutes, all without leaving the comfort of your chair.

Disadvantages: Too many choices can lead to decision paralysis. Try to narrow down your choices as much as possible.

 You can search for a journal based any aspect of your paper, such as the main topic, the discipline, types of participants or population, the approach or types of methods used in the research among others.

The bottom line is, any of these approaches can yield several journals that might consider publishing your paper. That can be either a good thing, or a confusing conundrum. I suggest that you use any combination of these approaches to best suit your needs. As you start your search for a suitable journal for your eventually-published paper, set out to narrow your choices down to no more than three finalists.

Look at the Instructions for Authors of all three of the finalist journals. Print them out and read them carefully. Share them with your coauthors. Consider their opinions. You may already have a clear winner for a journal, which is great as you start writing, because then you can format the paper based on the instructions for authors from the very beginning of your writing.

If you are still undecided at this stage, this should not impede your progress in writing a good paper. File the instructions for authors of the journals that you are considering in a folder, and revisit it as you progress in your writing. Something will pop up as you move along the process of writing, and the right journal will become obvious to you.

As a final recourse in making the decision about which journal to choose, you can write an email to the editors-in-chief of the journals that you are considering. Ask if they think the paper you are writing is suitable for their journal. If you decide to do this, it would be helpful to include a very good, almost final abstract of your paper in your email.

The impact factor

Not all journals are created equal. Some journals are considered more prestigious and have a better reputation than others, and this should be considered when making your selection. Some of the most respected scientists have only a few publications in the most prestigious journals. This is regarded as equivalent to, or even more valuable than, having many publications in journals of little prestige. Some of the more prestigious journals are *Science*, *Nature* and *Cell*. One of the best ways to determine the prestige of a journal is to consider its impact factor.

The prestige of the journal is not a subjective measure; it can actually be quantified. Prestige is determined by several factors; the most important is known as the impact factor.

The journal impact factor is a measure of the frequency an <u>average article</u> in a journal is cited in other articles in a given year. The impact factor is an indicator of a journal's relative importance compared to others, because it is a measure of its influence on the scientific community. It is important to note that the impact factor does not measure why the articles were cited in other papers. It is possible that a paper could be cited in other papers in a negative way, perhaps as other authors are trying to refute a finding. But for the most part, papers are cited in the literature as supporting evidence. Thus, the impact factor is considered the best estimate of the level of influence of a paper on the works of others.

The impact factor for a journal is calculated by dividing the number of current-year citations to articles published in the two previous years by the total number of articles published in the two previous years. For example:

How the impact factor is calculated:

To calculate the 2015 impact factor for the (fictitious) *Journal of Critical Findings*, the number of times that papers published in the journal were cited in other publications during the previous two years would be totaled. Let's say the total number of citations to all 72 papers published by the journal were 550. The impact factor for 2015 would be 550/72 = 7.64.

Journal Citation Reports (JCR) is where you can find the largest repository of journal impact factors. The JCR publishes impact factors using citation data drawn from thousands of scholarly and technical journals produced by more than 3,000 publishers in over 60 countries. It includes virtually all specialties in the areas of science, technology, and social sciences.

Journal Citation Reports is an online citation indexing system published by Thomson Reuters. Thomson Reuters also publishes Web of Science, from where you can access a collection of other databases including BIOSIS Citation Index, Current Contents and SciElo.

Unlike PubMed, which is free, Web of Science and JCR require a subscription for access. If you are a member of a medical research center, it is very likely that your library already subscribes to this service. If you don't have access to a medical library, you can find impact factors in other ways. For example, many journals now include their impact factor in their "About" page as part of their description of the journal. Sometimes, if you google the name of the journal that you are interested in and the words "impact factor" you may also be able to find the number. In addition, some entities publish a list of older impact factors, but these are generally unsearchable and unreliable. Beware of other companies that offer you access to journal impact factors for a fee. They are often scams.

The problem with finding the impact factors for journals individually instead of searching through JCR is that you would not be able to do a comparative search. One of the most valuable aspects of the JCR search engine is that you can search using a word or phrase, and you will be able to see all of the indexed journals that have that word or phrase in one list.

In this way, you can compare the journals side-by-side, allowing you to consider a broader set of journals. You will be able to determine how the journals that you are considering rank among others in the same area or discipline. This can be important as you should aim to publish in journals with the best impact factors that are realistic for your papers.

Again, if you have access to a medical library, it is very likely that they have a paid subscription to Web of Science. Ask your librarian or IT personnel for access information.

Once on the website, choose the tab labeled *Journal Citation Reports* at the top of the page. This will take you to the InCites^{TM} Journal Citation Reports^{R} where you can find journal impact factors of all journals indexed in the system. You can search the system from here directly by journal name, category, etc.

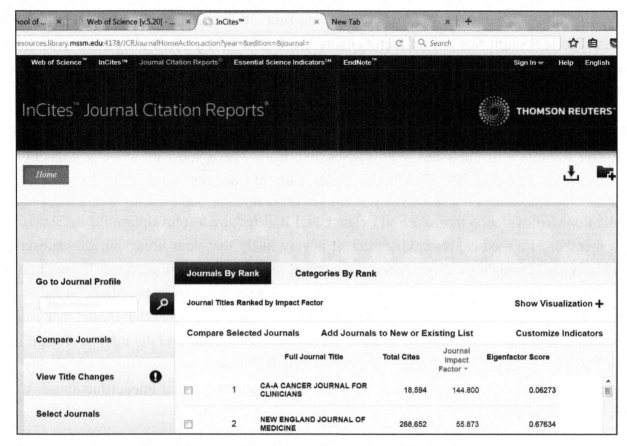

Figure 2: Landing page of Journal Citation Reports

The most useful way to use this platform, at least from my perspective, is to use the tool "Compare Journals". Click on that on the left side of the panel and it will take you to the next page where you can search for the specific journals that you are considering.

On the Compare Journals page, you will be able search the journals using any words or phrases that appear on the title. On this page, select "Trends". Then select the latest year for which data is available. Then, for Journal Metrics, select JIF (Journal Impact factor).

Once you have everything set up as above, you can click on "Select Journals", which will open a new window as illustrated in the next screen.

So, for example, I wanted to compare three journals that all happen to have the phrase "Environmental Health" in the title. By entering this phrase in the search box, 18 journal name choices appeared. For illustration purposes, I chose the first three journal names, which then appear on a separate box. Clicking "Submit" will give you a graph with the impact factors for each of the journals selected.

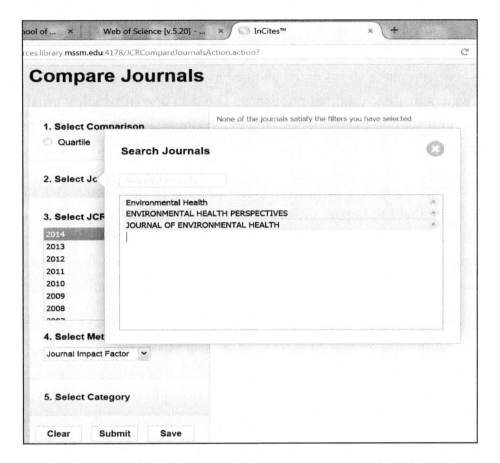

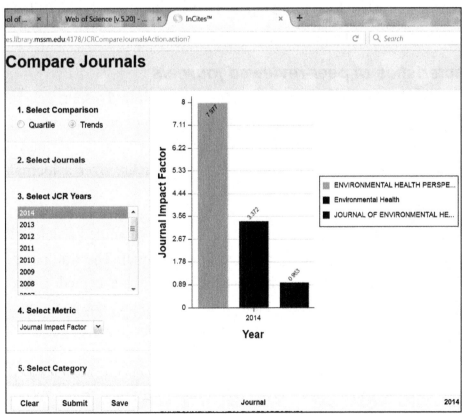

Figure 3: Comparing journals using Journal Citation Reports

As you can see, Environmental Health Perspectives has the highest impact factor. This may mean two things for me, either this is the perfect journal for my paper, or it is totally out of reach. This is where you make an informed choice based on experience and on keen observation of the types of papers that each journal publishes. The decision of which journal to choose also depends on your ability to be totally honest and determine the level of your paper, its potential impact and fit in the realm of journal choices.

If you further explore Journal Citation Reports, you will notice a number of patterns. For instance, you will see that the impact factors of the top journals are many times higher than the average. Publishing in one of these journals, such as Lancet or Nature, will be one of the most important accomplishments of your career. Increasingly, impact factors are used in the *curriculum vitae* of academic researchers as a measure of the quality of their publication records.

In the early years of the use of impact factors, there was discussion among faculty (especially those who were members of appointments and promotions committees) because impact factors skew higher in the cellular and molecular sciences. Other fields, such as the social sciences, tend to have lower impact factors. Most A&P committees now understand this phenomenon and take it into consideration when reviewing your publication record. There is increasing awareness that the impact factor of a researcher's bibliography must be interpreted within the context of their field.

Other characteristics of peer-reviewed journals

In the first paragraphs of the Instructions for Authors you will find a short general description of the journal that may include the frequency of publication (monthly, bimonthly), publisher, and other such information. This information is important; for example, you may favor a journal published monthly to get your article considered more quickly over a journal that publishes biannually.

Also, it is useful to look at the average turnaround time for submitted articles. To find this out, look at articles that have been recently published in the journal. The title page for each article should have the date of submission and the date the paper was accepted. Compare these dates with the date that the paper was actually published. This should give you a pretty good idea of how much time you would have to wait after submitting your paper to get a response from the journal.

Why is time-to-publication important? Well, if you are in a hurry to get something published quickly (perhaps you are being considered for a promotion) choosing a journal with a long wait time may not be a good idea. There are many factors that can affect a journal's wait time, including the number of submissions that they receive, the frequency of publication, the number of articles they publish per issue, the efficiency of the editorial staff, and the time it takes for the roster of reviewers to submit their critiques.

Some journals publish accepted articles online first in order to shorten the publication wait time for authors and to make their articles more readily available. These online preliminary publications are called "Epub" or "Ahead of print" and are citable in your *curriculum vitae* because they have already passed the peer review process and have been accepted by the journal. So, as part of your decision-making process, check to see if the journal you are considering offers fast electronic publication ahead of print.

Points to remember from Chapter 7

- There are a number of methods to use for choosing a journal:

  - The "follow the clues" approach requires that you pay close attention to the journals that have published many of the articles that you tend to cite in order to determine what journals your intended audience reads.
  - The "walk to the library approach" has you actually physically getting off your desk and going to the library to look at the journals that are organized by topic. You may also talk with a librarian who can do a more detailed search for potential journals.
  - The "let your fingers do the walking" approach requires the use of an online search tool such as PubMed to find journals in your area of interest. It is important that you narrow down your list of potential journals to those that realistically would publish your paper while still having the highest level of prestige that you can reach.

- The journal's impact factor is a measure of the number of times that papers in a journal are cited in other papers. It is published by Journal Citation Reports, a paid service created by Web of Science. Many journals also disclose their impact factor on their "About" page. Journal Citation Reports allows you to compare a number of journals based on their impact factor.

- In addition to their impact factor, journals vary on their time-to-publication, intended audiences, the kinds of papers they publish and other characteristics. You should assess all of these characteristics as part of the process of deciding where to submit your paper.

Additional Resources

CWTS Journal Indicators – www.journalindicators.com provides free access to bibliometric indicators on 20,000 journals and tries to normalize the impact factor variability between disciplines.

Google Scholar – https://scholar.google.com has added metrics to rank publications from websites that follow Google's inclusion guidelines. It also includes some conference articles and preprints. It could be used as an alternative to JCR, except the metrics are not as clear.

Other discipline-specific journal-ranking services include www.harzing.com for journals in economics, finance, accounting, management and marketing. Also, the European Science Foundation at www.esf.org ranks journals in humanities.

Exercise 7a: Analyze your options for potential journals

Compare three journals that you are considering.

Example, for illustration purposes only.

Journal 1: *Journal of Effects and Consequences*   **Impact Factor:**   *5.6*

1. What is the intended readership of this journal?

Statisticians and computer scientists. Members of the Society of Effects and Consequences.

2. What is the focus or theme of this journal?

Publication of statistical methods. Education and training of statisticians on these methods. Methods for proving and disproving experimental outcomes. Use of statistical methods in new settings and applications.

3. Circle the kind of paper you are intending to write: Review, Commentary, Case Report, Original Research, Meta-analysis? Does this journal publish this kind of paper? ____No   _X___Yes

4. Examine the list of editors. Are there any names of researchers in your field? Is there anyone you know or whose work you follow? If so, list them here:

Dr. Maria C. Marta, University of Lara, works on computational methods for evidence-based science.

5. Examine recent publications. Are there any papers similar to yours? If so, what would your paper add to the current literature?

Marta MC et al, 2013. A new method to test the consequences of action A on small datasets with multiple sources. J Effects & Conseq Vol 123: 555-570   They showed a method that only worked with small datasets of 10 or fewer data points, but ours can be used on databases of any size.

6. Time to publication of some recent sample articles in the journal (within the last two years of publication).

Article	Date submitted	Date accepted	Month published	Number of months to publication
1	1/2/13	10/5/13	11/13	11 months
2	3/13/14	8/1/14	11/14	8 months
3	8/4/13	2/8/14	6/14	10 months
4	1/18/14	8/19/14	10/14	10 moths
				Average number of months: 9.75

7. Pros of publishing in this journal   Cons of publishing in this journal

I am a member of the Society	Has a slower time to publication than Journal #2
It has the highest impact factor in the field	It is not open access
Has the best audience for this paper	It has a word limit of only 1,000 words for original research papers

Exercise 7b: Analyze your options for potential journals: Journal 1

Compare three journals that you are considering. Write your options here:

Journal 1: _____   Impact Factor: _____

1. **What is the intended readership of this journal?**

   _____

   _____

   _____

2. **What is the focus or theme of this journal?**

   _____

   _____

   _____

   _____

3. **Circle the kind of paper are you intending to write, i.e., Review, Commentary, Case Report, Original Research, Meta-analysis? Does this journal publish this kind of paper?**

   _____No   _____Yes

4. **Examine the list of editors. Are there any names of researchers in your field? Is there anyone you know or whose work you follow? If so, list them here:**

   _____

   _____

   _____

   _____

5. **Examine recent publications. Are there any papers similar to yours? If so, what would your paper add to the current literature?**

   _____

   _____

   _____

   _____

6. Time to publication of some recent sample articles in the journal.

Article	Date submitted	Date accepted	Month published	Number of months to publication
1				
2				
3				
4				
				Average: months

7.

Pros of publishing in this journal	Cons of publishing in this journal

You may go to www.drluzclaudio.com and download the forms for the following exercises, which you will be able to customize to fill in.

Exercise 7c: Analyze your options for potential journals: Journal 2

Compare three journals that you are considering. Write your options here:

Journal 2: _____   Impact Factor: _____

1. What is the intended readership of this journal?

   _____

   _____

   _____

2. What is the focus or theme of this journal?

   _____

   _____

   _____

   _____

3. Circle the kind of paper are you intending to write, i.e., Review, Commentary, Case Report, Original Research, Meta-analysis? Does this journal publish this kind of paper?

   _____No   _____Yes

4. Examine the list of editors. Are there any names of researchers in your field? Is there anyone you know or whose work you follow? If so, list them here:

   _____

   _____

   _____

   _____

   _____

   _____

5. Examine recent publications. Are there any papers similar to yours? If so, what would your paper add to the current literature?

   _____

   _____

   _____

6. Time to publication of some recent sample articles in the journal.

Article	Date submitted	Date accepted	Month published	Number of months to publication
1				
2				
3				
4				
				Average: months

7. Pros of publishing in this journal   **Cons of publishing in this journal**

You may go to www.drluzclaudio.com and download the forms for the following exercises, which you will be able to customize to fill in.

Exercise 7d: Analyze your options for potential journals: Journal 3

Compare three journals that you are considering. Write your options here:

Journal 3: _____   Impact Factor: _____

1. What is the intended readership of this journal?

   _____

   _____

   _____

2. What is the focus or theme of this journal?

   _____

   _____

   _____

   _____

3. Circle the kind of paper are you intending to write, i.e., Review, Commentary, Case Report, Original Research, Meta-analysis? Does this journal publish this kind of paper?

   _____No   _____Yes

4. Examine the list of editors. Are there any names of researchers in your field? Is there anyone you know or whose work you follow? If so, list them here:

   _____

   _____

   _____

   _____

   _____

   _____

5. Examine recent publications. Are there any papers similar to yours? If so, what would your paper add to the current literature?

   _____

   _____

   _____

6. Time to publication of some recent sample articles in the journal.

Article	Date submitted	Date accepted	Month published	Number of months to publication
1				
2				
3				
4				
				Average: months

7. Pros of publishing in this journal   Cons of publishing in this journal

You may go to www.drluzclaudio.com and download the forms for the following exercises, which you will be able to customize to fill in.

Chapter 8: Ready, Set, Write!

"Inspiration comes from working every day."
— **Charles Baudelaire, 19th century French poet and essayist.**

The title of this chapter is misleading, really… In reality, I do not advise you to wait until all your data is in neat, beautiful figures and tables and all your reference material organized in lovely color-coded folders in order to start writing. Perhaps this chapter should be titled: "***Write, Ready, Set, Re-Write***".

In fact, you should be writing at every stage of your research process. When you are developing and executing your experiments, you should be writing your Materials and Methods section to ensure that you don't miss or forget any of the steps of your work. Your paper should be written in real time. Write as you conduct your work, even if your results are not yet final. Then, once you have final results, you may need to re-write or edit sections of your paper, especially when your data turns out to be surprising or unexpected.

As you come along in your career, you will notice that in reality you should be writing all the time. It is unlikely that there will be one fine day when you suddenly sit and start writing. It is more likely that you will have papers at different stages of completion. So, for instance, you might be writing the introduction for one paper while responding to reviewer critiques for another paper on the same day. Each writing project will blend with the next and the work will become easier.

You will reuse some of the literature cited in one paper in another… Writing research papers is a continuous process that does not have a beginning, and it may not have an end.

However, for the purpose of simplicity, and to be able to explain the process to you, we are starting from the top as if there is really a beginning—the paper's title. But keep in mind that writing your research paper is a process that will involve much writing and rewriting. Adapt the process outlined in this book to each of the papers that you will write along the way.

The writer's mindset

After selecting the journal, collecting background literature, and completing a comprehensive outline, you will be ready to put pen to paper (or fingers to keyboard, as the case may be). You have your outline in front of you, you have your files organized according to your outline, and you have easy access to your data figures and tables. The computer screen is on.

Where do you start?

When you sit in front of your computer to write, don't think, "Now, I am going to write my paper." This thought just makes the task seem overwhelming. You may experience serious writer's block at this point and end up staring blankly at your computer screen. Don't do that!

Instead, keep this thought in mind: "Now, I am going to write this subsection of the paper." Nothing else.

Each subtopic is clearly and concisely defined in your outline, and all the materials for each topic should already be neatly filed in your organizing system for that particular subtopic.

 All you need to do now is to set aside the small amount of time required to pull out the files containing the materials for that subtopic, review the contents and thoroughly digest the information. Only then will you begin to write. Each subtopic within each section should be only one to a few paragraphs long. Writing a few paragraphs per sitting is much more doable than sitting with the mindset of intending to write the whole paper.

An additional advantage to this technique is that you will have all the materials within reach for that particular subtopic, so you can make sure that the facts that you are citing actually do correspond to the findings since you can corroborate everything as you move along.

Also, you will have the references handy; these can be easily entered into the reference section as you write your text. No more asking yourself: "Where did I read about such and such a fact?" Take advantage of having the original sources right in front of you and cite them accurately as you go.

When you get in front of your computer to write, you should set yourself up to win and to accomplish your intended goal for that writing session. This is also made easier when you have a good outline. Every time that you make time to sit and write, you should look at your outline and decide which section would be the easiest to write at that moment.

Perhaps you have a complete set of papers to cite for that particular section, or you recently went to a seminar that gave you an idea of how to organize that section. In order words, once you have your outline, you don't have to do things in order. Do what comes easier first; this will help you build momentum for writing the more difficult parts of the paper.

You should also set yourself up to have efficient writing sessions by ensuring that you have everything that you need at hand. Here is a list of things you will need.

 What you need to have handy for setting up your writing space

- ✓ **Data figures, graphs and tables**
- ✓ **Instructions for authors of target journal**
- ✓ **Outline and reference materials**
- ✓ **Instrumental music and earphones**
- ✓ **Timer**
- ✓ **Pens, color markers (if using paper files)**
- ✓ **Something to drink (water, tea)**
- ✓ **Set email, facebook and all other notifications to OFF**

The horror of the blank page

The computer's white page should be accompanied by music from the shower scene of *Psycho*. It can be intimidating and sometimes downright scary to stare at the abyss of the blank page, but remember that you can use the outline as a template to get the writing started.

To do this, just open up the outline on your screen and start filling in the sections using the headings and subheadings that you have already created. You can delete any numbering or indentations later. The important thing is to have something to get you started.

Using the outline as a template has several advantages. One is that of course, you would not be staring at a blank page. There should already be significant writing done—your annotated outline should already be complete and contain much of your needed information.

Another advantage is that the outline will serve as a map to guide you all the way through the process of writing the paper. You will be able to see where you are going with your writing. You will also be able to knock out the sections that might be easy for you to write. For instance, you may have some text on the same topic that you previously used in a grant proposal or in a seminar presentation. Using the outline as a template will help you realize how much work you already have done.

To multitask *or* to batch?

The writing process requires organization—not only of your physical space and materials, but also your brain. With so many things to do in a day, deadlines, interests and projects screaming for attention, carving out time to write can seem like an onerous task.

Writing requires your full attention, but it does not necessarily require an exorbitant amount of time. One key to effective writing is having focused intention. A big impediment to successful writing is constantly switching from writing to meeting with colleagues, to doing data analysis. Every time you switch from one activity to the next, you waste time by redirecting your attention elsewhere. This is because it takes your brain some time to adjust to different types of activities, which makes it difficult focus and get into a productive rhythm.

This constant switching from one type of task to another also prevents you from getting in a groove that allows your work to come freely with minimal effort. It is not the most productive way to use your time.

This is why the idea of multitasking is so flawed. Even though we may think that we are doing two or more tasks at the same time, in reality we are merely switching from one task to the other. It has been shown by Peter Bregman from the Harvard Business Review that productivity is reduced 40% when multitasking. Trying to do too many things at once leads to decreased production.

A better approach to getting things done is batching—the process of grouping like-activities together. For instance, when you set aside time to do a literature search for your introduction, you should also look for the citations that you will need for your other sections. It will save you a lot of time if you stay within a single activity, rather than switching back and forth between literature search, writing, talking to colleagues, etc.

Play beat the clock

This is my secret weapon for increasing my writing productivity. There's absolutely no other tip that speeds up your writing output that works as well as this one.

Have you noticed how the pressure of having a deadline helps you stay on task and focused? Mostly because you HAVE to do it? Your boss hands you a database at 4PM and asks you to finish it in an hour for a grant deadline. Suddenly, a task that would have normally taken you three hours to complete takes you one hour. What if you could bottle up that kind of focused motivation and drink it up whenever you need it?

You can.

You can recreate that kind of focus by giving yourself mini-deadlines, racing to meet them and rewarding yourself when you do.

For example, let's say that you decide that you have all the information you need to write the first two paragraphs of the introduction. You have everything handy in your folders and the annotated outline on your computer screen. Decide how long it will take you to write that section. Suppose that you decide it will be 45 minutes. Set up a timer (you can use a lab timer or one on your computer or phone). Start the timer and go at it. Race the clock to complete the task in the amount of time allotted.

This technique has served me well for years. I hit the mark almost every time, because by now I have a good idea of how long each writing task will take. But at first, you may overestimate or underestimate the time that you will need to complete each writing session. That is okay. It is part of the process of learning about yourself.

You should set up the timer to an amount of time that is comfortable but challenging. This should always be less than two hours, because your body needs periodic rests. At the end of each timed writing session, you should feel a little tired, but also well accomplished and satisfied with your work. Make sure to notice that feeling and acknowledge it. Take a few minutes to breathe and realized that it was work well done.

When I complete a timed writing session in the time I allotted, I usually reward myself with a short walk, a stretch, a nice piece of chocolate … anything that will send my brain a signal that I did a good job and motivate me to do it again.

Estimating the right amount of time comes from experience. At first, you will be way off the mark, estimating too little or too much time for completing a writing section. But as you practice, you will get better and better at it.

Play beat the calendar

Have you noticed that whenever you have a deadline imposed by someone else, you never miss it? While if the deadline is merely a goal that you have created for yourself, you rarely complete it on time?

This is because we give priority to the commitments that we have with others, while neglecting our own to-do list.

Here are some ideas how you can address this:

- Put your deadline on your calendar and make a formal commitment with yourself to keep it.

- Set a deadline with your coauthors. This is especially effective if your coauthors are supervisors or senior collaborators. Even though you are the one setting the deadline, you will be compelled to meet that person's expected date of completion.

- Create your own negative consequences for missing deadlines. Some negative consequences that you can self-impose could include refraining from desserts or sweets until you meet the deadline. Although some people find these kinds of consequences effective motivating tools, I personally don't believe in self-punishment because I don't think it's nearly as effective as positive reinforcement. If used repeatedly, I think that self-punishment could actually backfire to the point where you may start resenting your writing sessions. Thus, I suggest that you use this technique for increasing your motivation sparingly.

Adopting a writing habit

Most scientists first go into the field because they love the act of discovery, being in the lab or on the field, conducting experiments, making direct observations and collecting data. As they progress up the academic ladder, many are surprised that most of their time is spent writing on a computer and very little time s spent actually doing the things they love.

The nature of the way scientific studies are conducted requires investigators to write and write, more and more. Grants and research papers are the main outcomes by which our productivity is measured.

 Getting a writing habit early in your career will help you to get ahead in your profession.

To create a writing habit, my suggestion to you is to spend some quiet time creating your ideal weekly schedule. On a planner, carefully input the things that you have to do regularly, such as attending prescheduled recurrent seminars, teaching or taking classes, attending workshops and leading laboratory meetings.

Then, fill in the things that are necessary but are not time sensitive. This would include conducting experiments in the lab, meeting with community collaborators and conducting data analyses. Include time for writing in this MUST-DO list.

For scheduling your writing time, ask yourself these questions: What is the ideal time of day for writing? When is my space (lab, office) most quiet? When do I usually feel most focused? What day of the week do I have some nice blocks of uninterrupted time to write?

Add some fun into this <u>ideal</u> week. Set time for having lunch with friends, taking a walk in a park, or whatever quick thing you might want to do that gives you a jolt of energy to continue enjoying your ideal week and enjoying your work life.

Depending on how structured your days are, you may or may not want to schedule specific times for writing. For instance, I like to write my papers right after I arrive at the office. This works for me because it sends my brain and my staff the signal that says, "Writing is so important to me that it is the first thing I must do in the day."

I typically arrive at the office early. It is quiet and there are fewer interruptions from others. This may work for you, or it may not. For you, it may work best to write right after lunch, or you may feel particularly inspired to write after lab group meetings. Whenever the best time is for you, make it a habit to always write at that time or close to that time.

Note that when I say "time" here, it does not necessarily mean the hour or time on the clock. It tends to be most effective to set the time to write for after you do something else. So for example, I like to write right after I arrive at the office, regardless of what time I actually get there. For you, it may be more convenient to set your writing time for after lunch or for after you attend that department seminar.

The idea is to program your brain to expect to write after a certain stimulus has taken place. This action will help in forming and reinforcing your writing habit. After a couple of months, you will find it easier and easier to make it an automatic part of your routine rather than something that you have to spend energy deciding to do.

 __Work on creating a writing habit by anchoring it after a positive and consistent trigger, and a small but noticeable self-reward after accomplishing a writing goal.__

Points to remember from Chapter 8

- To get into a writing mindset, you must consciously create a writing space that will promote your focus, concentration and comfort. Setting up a writing space (whether a corner of a lab bench, a favorite spot at the library or a dining table at home) will promote a good writing mindset. Ensure that you have everything you need at this space.

- Decide that writing and publishing is an important priority in your professional life. As such, you must allocate sufficient time to accomplish this goal.

- Try to batch your work into chunks of when you are doing something that is similar or that naturally goes together. Multitasking is counterproductive when it comes to writing for scientific publication.

- Take control of your clock and your calendar. Create mini-deadlines for yourself and take them seriously. Schedule writing time into your schedule and make your schedule public and official. Make this writing time just as firm as going to classes or seminars.

- Get into a writing habit. Use self-rewards as motivators for completing writing tasks.

- Design your ideal weekly schedule to include writing time as well as fun time. Aim every day to meet that ideal as closely as possible.

Additional Resources

Allen, David. *Getting Things Done: The Art of Stress-Free Productivity*. Penguin Publishing, 2015

Exercise 8a: *Where does my time go?*

Keep track of your work-related activities during a typical week (Typical, meaning that you are not traveling or doing anything out of the ordinary). Do not try to change anything about your day. Just observe and record the number of hours spent on each activity (to the nearest half hour).

Example from the log from an assistant professor

ACTIVITY	Mon	Tue	Wed	Thu	Fri	Sat/ Sun	Total hours /activity	Percent of work week
Experiments/ data collection	0	1	1	0	0	0	2	3.8%
Data analysis, graphing and visualization	1	2	0	0	2	0	5	9.4%
Lectures, classes, seminars	0	1	0	0	1	0	2	3.8%
Reading/ searching the literature	1	1	0	0	0	2	4	7.5%
Meetings with colleagues, networking	0.5	1	1	0	0	0	2.5	4.7%
Teaching, tutoring mentoring	0	2	2	2	3	0	9	16.9%
Administrative duties such as orders & budgets	1	0	1	0.5	.5	0	3	5.7%
Writing grant proposals	2	1.5	2	2.5	3	0	11	20.8%
Writing papers for publication	2	0	2.5	3	2	3	12.5	23.6%
Other Planned seminar	1	0	0	1	0	0	2	3.8%
Total hours worked	8.5	9.5	9.5	9.0	11.5	5	53*	100%

*Use this number to calculate the percentage of time that you spend on each activity

Exercise 8b: Where does my time go?

Keep track of your work-related activities:

Date:

ACTIVITY	Mon	Tue	Wed	Thu	Fri	Sat/ Sun	Total hours /activity	Percent of work week
Experiments/ data collection								
Data analysis, graphing and visualization								
Lectures, classes, seminars								
Reading/ searching the literature								
Meetings with colleagues, networking								
Teaching, tutoring mentoring								
Administrative duties such as orders & budgets								
Writing grant proposals								
Writing papers for publication								
Other								
Total hours worked							*	

*Use this number to calculate the percentage of time that you spend on each activity

You may go to www.drluzclaudio.com and download the forms for the following exercises, which you will be able to customize to fill in.

Chapter 9: Writing Your Paper

"The universe is made of stories, not of atoms."

—Muriel Rukeyser, American poet and political activist who wrote about environmental and occupational issues and social justice.

Congratulations, you are ready to write! It probably seems like forever ago when you started preparing for your writing journey, but I assure you that all the preparation you have done will make the writing process much easier. Even though you may now feel like you are just starting, you are actually half-way there—that is, if you have done all the work in the previous chapters.

Let's review what we have done so far.

- Gained an understanding of the importance of writing and publishing research papers, and developed a sense of urgency for adopting strategies that will lead to efficient writing and publishing,

- Organized the data and decided on the best ways to illustrate it for an article,

- Determined whether the data is ready to be published,

- Understood the different types of research papers and gathered ideas for different publication options,

- Presented preliminary data at professional conferences and seminars,

- Consulted and received feedback from colleagues,

- Created an annotated and detailed outline of the paper,

- Learned how to choose a journal,

- Learned how to increase writing efficiency and motivation to incorporate writing as part of weekly tasks.

Now, the time has come to write. All of the previous work has led to this.

Where should I start?

The simple answer is: at the beginning. The title page is the first page of the paper, and it should include the following:

- The title

- The names of all authors in the order they should appear (more on this later)

- The institutions with which each of the authors is affiliated

- Other information such as word count and abbreviations used throughout the manuscript may be included depending on the requirements of the journal; carefully check the Instructions for Authors for additional information that must be included on the title page.

If you have authors from more than one institution, use superscripted numbers next to their names and list their respective institutions as footnotes on the title page. You should also indicate the name of the **corresponding author** and include his or her full contact information. The corresponding author is the person who will receive all communications from the journal and will be asked to respond to reviewers' comments and other queries.

Some journals require additional information on the title page, such as a **short title**. The short title is an abbreviated title that will be used as a running head on the pages when the paper is published.

You may also be asked to include **key words**. These are words or phrases that will be used for indexing your paper in *Index Medicus* or in other such search engines. It is important to choose key words that are not included in your title. The words in the title are automatically included as parameters in the search engine, so having those as key words would be redundant.

Another piece of information that may be included on the title page is the **word count**. This is the total number of words in the paper, which will help the typesetter design the journal issues. Always check the journal's instructions for authors or submission instructions to determine what information must be provided on the title page.

What's next?

Even though your outline follows the order of the sections as required by most journals (Abstract, Introduction, Materials and Methods, Results, Discussion), I recommend writing the sections in this order:

First

Materials and Methods – You should be writing this section while conducting your research – in real time. If you don't write as you do the work, you will have to retrace your steps, making you more prone to error.

Once you are finally settled into writing your paper, you will find it helpful to begin with this section because it is easy. You are simply describing HOW you did it. Describe the important supplies and the processes used in conducting your research. This should be easy because you already know the information for this section better than anyone.

Another good reason to start with the Materials and Methods section is that writing <u>anything</u> will serve as traction to drive you forward in your writing. Additionally, as you recount what was done to complete the research, you may realize that an author needs to be included or excluded as their contributions become more apparent. It is important to establish authorship early on.

Second

Introduction - This section explains WHY the research was conducted. It contains background information, some of which you probably already have in other writings such as in a grant proposal. Remember, the introduction doesn't describe everything about your topic; you should focus instead on setting the stage and providing the rationale for your study. What other literature led you to undertake the project presented in your paper?

Third

Results - This is the real meat of the paper. It recounts WHAT was discovered. Writing this section will allow you to see the significance of your research.

Fourth

Discussion – This is the SO WHAT of your paper. This explains your data and compares it with the existing literature. It puts things into context. The discussion of each result should be written in the same order as it is presented in the Results section, and thus should follow it very closely.

Fifth

Abstract – The abstract should reflect exactly what is presented in the paper. Therefore, writing it first may be a waste of time unless you are working from an abstract that was previously published or presented at a conference. If you are working from an existing abstract, you should go back to it after you have finished your paper to make sure that it still reflects the paper's contents.

All the time   **References** – You should enter your referenced material as you write. No matter what method you use for capturing and inputting citations, you should add literature references throughout the writing process, rather than at the end because this will ensure that you will cite the correct papers for the assertions that you make as you write. If not, it can be easy to forget where you found a piece of information or a factual statement.

Although this order is my strong suggestion, some of this is a matter of preference. Some authors may be more comfortable writing their sections in the order they will appear in the paper, or in another order altogether. You should choose the order that works best for you. The important thing is to start, continue and finish writing your paper.

Writing in a logical order: The funnel

One way to organize your writing is referred to as the *deductive method* of organization. Deductive method starts with presenting broad or *general* information and moves on to more *specific* information. This is a logical and systematic method for organizing your thoughts that provides a clear vision for writing. The deductive method is a tool for distilling your writing down to its conclusion. It can be visualized as a funnel onto which you pour the larger ideas and as you write, you distill out the more detailed pieces of information until you arrive to the logical conclusions.

The deductive method will help move your writing forward. Use it to organize each section, each subsection and even each paragraph of your paper. Each funnel will be composed of mini-funnels, each having the same organizing principle: from general "thesis statement" to specific "evidence". Remember, the poetry of your paper is in its logical flow, systematic approach, clarity and consistency.

When writing your paper, you should think about what the reader should know first. What should they know next? And next? The information should be presented so that it is easy to understand your results and key findings. You should always aim for clarity and directness, rather than obfuscation and complication.

 Follow a logical progression throughout your paper using the deductive method of organizing your narrative – from more general statements to the more specific. Do this for each section and subsection.

Organizing your paper is like building a pyramid. First, you lay down the foundation bricks. From there you add smaller, more detailed bricks. For example, an epidemiological study of asthma may first present the demographic characteristics of the whole population such as race, gender, age, income, etc. This would be followed by the asthma prevalence rates for each group in the population. Then comes the fine tuning—perhaps an analysis of the independent effects of each factor by providing odds ratios or another measure of association.

Keep in mind that this progression (from more general to more specific) may not necessarily follow the chronological order in which you actually conducted the experiments or observations. Sometimes there can be much back and forth in the way that scientific research is conducted. You should disregard the order in which you conducted your studies and try to keep in mind what your readers will need to know and in what order they need to know it. Help your readers understand bit by bit by writing the information in a logical order that presents the data progressively.

Use your outline as a template. Start the writing process by filling in the outline, using its headings and subheadings to prompt your writing. You can keep the headings on the draft paper or remove them depending on the journal requirements.

Writing the Materials and Methods section

I was taught the old fashion way when I was a graduate student. In those days, you wrote in a big, heavy lab notebook every day (one of those huge spiral-bound notebooks with the blue-lined graph paper). The notebook never ever left the lab bench, and we—the minions working on our PhDs—had to write in our notebooks what we did in the lab each day. Every experiment and every observation was recorded. We taped the labels of every new batch of cell culture media to the notebook to record a change of vendor. Observations from all experiments were detailed with drawings and diagrams—even the experiments that failed and the negative results were included. Every mistake, every wrong molarity calculation, every experiment conducted in triplicate; everything was recorded in the lab notebook, for posterity…

Now I understand my mentor's insistence on keeping diary-like lab notes. The first time I wrote a paper, the materials and methods section practically jumped out fully-formed from the lab notebook onto the page of my paper, which was published quickly and with few reviewers' critiques.

Even if you are now a long way past having a wonderfully demanding thesis mentor like mine, it pays to keep some good habits for detailed recording of your materials, methods and protocols as you go along conducting your experiments and collecting data. Do not trust your not-so-photographic memory when it comes to recalling what you did to arrive at your results. Keeping some kind of running record will not only save you time when writing for publication, but it will keep your methods accurate, give you clues as to what went wrong if something didn't quite make sense, and will go a long way towards keeping your reputation intact should your results be questioned in the future.

 The Materials and Methods section explains HOW you conducted this study. Use it to explain to other scientists the way you got it done.

As you already know, the Materials and Methods section is a description of exactly <u>how</u> the data was obtained. This section should contain enough detail to allow a competent scientist in your field to reproduce your work.

In order to achieve that level of accuracy while staying brief, the Materials and Methods section should include a description of the specific materials used. For example, if you conducted experiments on protein synthesis using a specific kind of bacterial cell line that is commercially available, you should include, in parentheses, the name and location of the company that supplied you with that cell line. This will allow other scientists to locate the company and order the same kind of bacteria you used for their own experiments.

In science, imitation is a high form of flattery. You want others to be able to do the same thing that you did in your research, and hopefully come up with similar observations confirming your results. Reproducibility is a cornerstone of scientific research.

 Write the Materials and Methods section in real-time, as you are conducting your research.

When writing the Materials and Methods section, start by describing the object of your investigation. If you studied a population of buffalo in the wild, describe their numbers, location, any selection criteria used to arrive to the study sample. If your work involved cell lines, describe their origin, the method of isolation and any additional properties. Start with the general description of the group of things that you studied, be it herds, human populations, laboratory animals, tissues, cells, compounds or molecules. Continue by recounting the different methods, processes, experiments and protocols used, and then end with a description of the data analysis methods used to make sense of it all.

Most journals allow the inclusion of subheadings in the Materials and Methods section. Using them wisely should be helpful to you in organizing your writing. If you created a strong outline, these subheadings should already be written, so you should be able to follow that as a template.

If you used methods that are detailed in other publications or already exist as standard procedures in your field, you can briefly summarize the method, and provide a reference to the paper where the method is detailed. One transitional phrase that is often used is, "In brief..." along with a brief description of the method and appropriate citation. For example, a paper that we published in 2006 used a protocol that we previously had detailed in a paper published in 1999. So our statement read (underlines added): *"Asthma hospitalization rates were determined for all zip codes of New York City. In brief, data from the New York State Department of Health was collected and analyzed using a geographical information system as previously described (Claudio et al, 1999)."* From Claudio *et al*, 2006.

 If you conducted a study of an educational asthma intervention in schools, your subheadings may be something like this:

- Population (location, age bracket, racial/ethnic composition…)

- Methods for selection of children with asthma

- Questionnaire content

- Description of asthma intervention protocol

- Clinical assessment methods

- Statistical analysis

Using a flow diagram to organize your Materials and Methods section

A flow diagram is a graphical representation of a sequence of actions or steps used to describe a process or a series of steps in a process. It shows what steps were taken to arrive at the resulting endpoints. Generally, flow diagrams make it easy to see how the sequence of steps was followed to arrive to an outcome.

I always use flow diagrams to conceptualize a study design, and often include them in grant proposals as a way to illustrate a summary of the research plan. But in recent years, I have seen flow diagrams being included in research papers or as supplementary documents to published research papers.

Flow diagrams are also helpful in presenting how a methods protocol was applied to yield a particular cohort in a clinical trial. If your paper is a clinical trial, you may need to provide a flow diagram of how the study participants were selected and assigned to the trial groups. A template of the flow diagram proposed by the Consolidated Standards of Reporting Trials or CONSORT is included below as a good example. More information about the CONSORT Statement can be found at: ***http://www.consort-statement.org***

Even if your paper is not a clinical trial, creating a flow diagram like this can help you conceptualize your experimental design and can be useful for explaining your methods, even if you do not include the diagram in your paper. Consider creating a flow diagram to help you organize the Materials and Methods section in a logical sequence, whether you decide to include it in the paper or not.

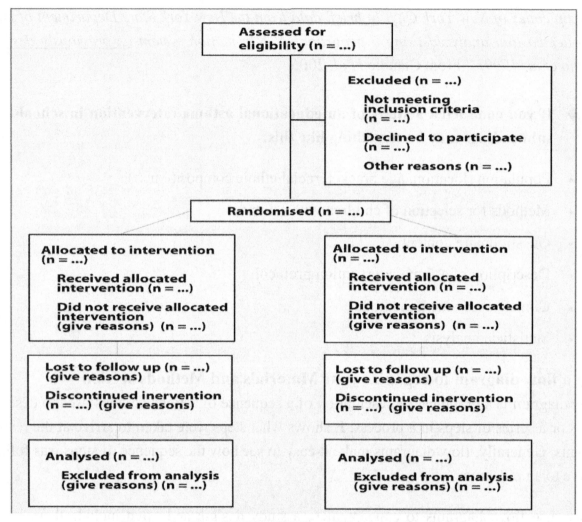

Figure 1: The CONSORT Flow-Diagram Template

From: Schulz KF, Altman DG, Moher D, for the CONSORT Group (2010) CONSORT 2010 Statement: Updated Guidelines for Reporting Parallel Group Randomized Trials. http://www.consort-statement.org/

 Protocols submitted within grant proposals and pilot projects can sometimes be adapted or edited for use in the Materials and Methods section of your paper.

Writing the Introduction

The introduction provides background information in a way that orients the reader to the topic in general and to your research in particular, setting the stage for the results that are to be presented. The Introduction presents the state-of-the-knowledge on the topic. It describes the scientific problem that you addressed in this research, and it briefly states the approach you used. It can state a hypothesis. It also offers a rationale that explains why you conducted this study.

 The INTRODUCTION section explains WHY you conducted this study. Use it to set the stage, and to present your rationale.

The literature used to build the Introduction is often composed of the kinds of papers your mentor may have given you when you first started working on this particular research question. This set of papers may have presented a broader perspective on your topic or led directly to the research that you conducted for the paper.

The key points to be presented in the Introduction are:

1. A definition of the scope of the problem. Explanation on why the study is important.

2. A brief review of the literature related to the central topic of the paper, including sufficient background that will help the reader understand why you embarked on this investigation.

3. A description of what knowledge exists in the field today and what still needs to be discovered. Include any knowledge gaps that you intend to fill in with your paper.

4. An explanation of the study's purpose and what questions your investigation addresses.

5. A brief hypothesis statement.

6. A brief description of the approach you took to address the research question.

Using your outline as a template is the easiest way to write your paper. Having those headings and subheadings on the screen will help you focus on each section, and you will know which files you need for each writing session. When you sit to write each section of the Introduction, access the papers that you have collected for each section and subsection, which should have been filed in paper or electronic folders labeled with each outline heading.

As you set aside time to write, intend to write just a subsection of the Introduction as defined in your outline, nothing more. Access the research papers that you had set aside for that subsection and begin to write with those papers right in front of you. As you write, remember the funnel (deductive writing) described previously.

Sit at your computer with ONLY the papers that you intend to include in the first paragraph of the introduction. Review them. Take notes. Organize your thoughts. Set a timer. Then, start writing. Here's what a first paragraph might look like:

Introduction The food environment plays an influential role in shaping the diets of children and may contribute to the development of obesity and other adverse health outcomes [1, 2]. Foods purchased outside the home, specifically at restaurants, tend to be energy dense and have low nutritional value. A previous study evaluated nearly 3,500 children's meal combinations offered at 34 of the top 50 restaurant chains in the United States (US), with respect to the National Restaurant Association's KidsLiveWell standards, which provide specifications for calories, total fat, saturated fat, trans fat, sodium, sugar, and inclusion of food groups (i.e. vegetables and fruits) [3]. The study found that 91 % of the meals did not meet the KidsLiveWell standards and over a quarter of the restaurants did not have any meals that met these standards [3]. This is of concern because restaurant food and fast-food are common in children's diets, contributing approximately 84–191 kcal and 160– 404 kcal to the mean daily intakes of children and adolescents, respectively, who reported being consumers [4]. A recent analysis of NHANES 2007–2010 showed that half of US children, ages 2–18 years, consumed fast-food and 10.5 % were high consumers, with more than 30 % of their daily calories coming from fast-food restaurants [5].

From: Deierlein AL, Peat K, Claudio L, 2015.

Note that the first sentence states the most important premise, ie, that the food environment contributes to obesity in children. Then, the argument is made that restaurant meals are a significant portion of this food environment and evidence is presented that restaurant meals are nutritionally deficient. This paragraph supports the assertion that it is important to study the contribution of restaurant meals to the food environment in children's diets. Note also that the paragraph includes a lot of specific information from other studies. For that reason, it was important to have those articles handy and to enter the references at the same time in order to accurately represent the supporting data from those articles.

Once you have written the first paragraph, check your timer. Did it take you more or less time than you estimated? Adjust your timer accordingly, and check to see if you have time to write your second paragraph. If so, write your second paragraph, again adding the corre-sponding citations as you go. Double-check the statements you are citing to ensure that they are actually what the literature says. This should be easy, since you have the relevant papers right in front of you from your outline files. Do not move onto another paragraph before adding your citations. Continue on like this, paragraph by paragraph.

The last paragraph of your introduction should naturally lead into the materials and methods section. This means that it should naturally and logically connect the previous statements of topic importance, current knowledge, and knowledge gaps right to a statement about what you have done to address the stated research question.

Here is an example of the last paragraph of the introduction from the same paper as the example above:

> There are currently no studies, to our knowledge, that evaluate the most recent changes in children's menus offered at both sit down and fast-food restaurant chains. The purpose of this study was to determine longitudinal changes in the nutrient and fruit/vegetable content of main and side dishes available on children's menus at popular US restaurant chains between 2010 and 2014. This time period approximately captures the introduction and pending implementation of the federal menu labeling law.
>
> From: Deierlein AL, Peat K, Claudio L, 2015

Notice the clear statement of objectives of the study, why the project was conducted in New York City and what will be presented in the rest of the paper.

Background sections from previous grant proposals can often be reworked, updated and used for some sections of your Introduction.

Writing the Results section

The Results section is the place where your data should shine. In order for that to happen, you must present it in the best light. This means creating awesome figures, graphs, tables, charts, photographs, plots, maps, diagrams or any other type of illustration that would best highlight the results of your research. The figures should speak for themselves. They need to convey lots of information. The figures and tables should be self-contained, meaning that a reader should be able

to look at a figure in your paper and understand what the results are without having to refer much to the text in the rest of the paper.

The text in the Results section should be straightforward, and should not repeat the information presented in the accompanying figures and tables. Instead, the text should present and point to the information shown in the figures and tables, and direct the reader to view the figures to gain information on a particular point being illustrated.

Thus, the text in the Results section should serve as a guided tour of what is illustrated in the figures and tables without duplicating the information. For this reason, it is important to use the right types of figures for the type of data you wish to present.

Before writing the results section, it is important to clearly understand your data and the message you are trying to present to your readers. Is the data discrete or continuous? Are you analyzing trends over time, or comparing parts of a whole? Should you present the precise values of the variables, or emphasize their relationship to other variables? The answers to these types of questions will help you determine the best way to present your data.

 The **RESULTS** section details **WHAT** you found through conducting this study. Use it to present to other scientists what you discovered in your research.

An example of a paragraph from the results section of one of our papers is included below. Notice a few things:

1. This section of the Results includes a subheading "Multivariate Analysis". This subheading comes directly from the outline.

2. The paragraph refers to Table 4 by providing a descriptive statement of what the table conveys.

3. Salient features of the table are detailed in the narrative in order to draw attention to those important findings. However, those findings are not detailed in the narrative, i.e., no results that are directly illustrated in the table are included in the text. Instead, include some results that can be derived from the table (For example: "Asians had almost a 40% lower risk…").

Multivariate Analysis

A logistic regression model was created to examine independent effects of demographic factors on current asthma (Table 4). Living in a low-income household, living in an area with high asthma hospitalization rates, and male gender were all independently associated with having current asthma. After controlling for ZIP Code grouping and income level, the relationship between race/ethnicity and current asthma disappeared, except in the case of Puerto Rican and Asian children. Regardless of where they lived or household income level, Puerto Ricans had the highest risk of current asthma, more than double that of White children. Conversely, Asians had almost a 40% lower risk of current asthma than did other ethnic groups.

Table 4.
Independent effects associated with Current asthma*

	OR	95 CI
Gender		
Male	1.53	1.19–1.97
Female	Reference	–
Ethnicity		
Dominican	1.65	.888–3.06
Mexican	.701	.325–1.52
Puerto Rican	2.28	1.40–3.72
Other Hispanic	1.23	.751–2.00
African-American	1.78	.994–3.19
Asian	.604	.391–.933
Other	1.74	.969–3.13
White	Reference	–
Income		
<$20,000	2.10	1.25–3.52
$20,001–$39,999	1.83	1.05–3.18
$40,000–$74,999	1.66	.896–3.06
$75,000 or more	Reference	–
Neighborhood ZIP Codes		
High	1.73	1.20–2.49
Median	.890	.544–1.45
Low	Reference	–

* Adjusted for age of child, although not significantly associated with current asthma (OR = .990, p = .777).

From: Claudio L, et al 2006.

Writing the Discussion

The Discussion section of the paper provides interpretation of the results and puts your results into the context of the existing literature. This is where you will compare your results with the data obtained by other investigators, and where you will attempt to explain why your data is similar or different than others. This section also offers meaningful insight regarding the significance of your results.

At the end of the Discussion, you may also include any conclusions made directly from your results and some recommendations for future directions if appropriate.

 *The **DISCUSSION** section is the **SO WHAT** of your study. Use it to compare and contrast your results with what has been published in the literature, and to distill the conclusions that can be derived from your interpretation of the results.*

In order to make sure that the Discussion is based exactly on the results that YOU obtained in THIS particular paper, divide the discussion section into subsections that follow the order of the data as it was presented in the Results section. Follow the same order that you used in the Results section and systematically go point-by-point, discussing each one as they were presented.

You don't necessarily need to include the same subheadings (many journals do not use subheadings in the discussion), but you can use the subheadings in your outline to help organize your thoughts and follow a logical progression in your writing. You can delete them later if the subheadings don't fit the journal's format.

Some key points to consider when writing the discussion include:

1. The Discussion serves to explain the results and draw conclusions. It should not be used to recapitulate or repeat the results already presented in the Results section.

2. In the Discussion, you should articulate how your results agree or disagree with findings in other published works.

3. You can include theoretical and practical implications of your work.

4. You should stick strictly to the facts presented by your results when drawing conclusions. Although some theoretical or speculative explanations may be presented in the Discussion, these must be based on the empirical data that you or others have observed.

5. Point out any exceptions. If your data doesn't fit with previous works, say so. Do not try to accommodate your data to fit what was expected.

6. Conclude with a bang! State the significance of your results using a balance of boldness and humility. Be clear and point out what your results may mean.

 Steps for writing the Discussion:

1. Have a printout of your Results section right next to your computer. For each of your results, write a phrase or statement that best describes the conclusion or meaning of each

of the results that you are presenting. As you review each result, ask yourself: "What does this result mean?" And, "What do I want the reader to understand from this result?"

2. Find in your outline files the papers that are related to each of the results. Review each of the papers to find the outcomes that can be compared with the work that you are presenting. Ask yourself, "How does their research compare to mine?" Or, "How is it similar or different?" Or, "Are their conclusions similar to mine?"

3. For each of the most salient outcomes of your research, write a paragraph stating your interpretation of the results and how those results compare to others. Include all appropriate references as you go along.

The Discussion section will be very satisfying for you to write. This is where you will have your results take their rightful place in the literature and where you can express the importance of your work. This is often where one realizes the actual meaning of the work. Enjoy this process!

 Notes from previous speaking engagements can often be reworked and included as part of your concluding statements at the end of the Discussion section.

Here is an example of the beginning paragraphs of a Discussion from one of my published papers:

Discussion

Prevalence of current asthma ranged from 6.39% to 17.9%, with an overall prevalence of 13.0%, more than twice recent estimates of national prevalence of 6.3% (13). In areas with the highest asthma hospitalization rates, more than one quarter of the children had ever received an asthma diagnosis. These ZIP Code areas were predominantly low-income minority communities. Even ZIP Code areas with very low asthma hospitalization rates and high numbers of nonminority residents had asthma prevalence at or above the national average. Therefore, although some neighborhoods bear a greater burden of disease than others, asthma is a critical health issue facing children throughout New York City.

Disparities in Asthma Prevalence Exist Among Urban Neighborhoods

Many studies have found higher-than-average childhood asthma prevalence in low-income minority communities, especially in urban settings 8, 14, 15, 16, 17, 18 and 19. However, it is not known what factors are the strongest contributors to the urban asthma epidemic. Certain race/ethnicity, income, and local environmental factors are considered culprits 18, 20, 21 and 22. In the present study, asthma prevalence is three times higher than the national average in communities consisting primarily of low-income minorities.

From Claudio et al, 2006

Notice that the Discussion states why the paper is important, and compares the results obtained with that of others. In this case, we included a subtitle that summarized a salient finding. This makes it easy for the readers to understand the main conclusions of the paper as they read along.

The conclusion can be incorporated into the writing of the Discussion or provided as a separate section that is marked with a heading. Some journals' instructions for authors request that the conclusion be marked with a heading, while others do not. If the journal does not require a separate conclusion section, I like to end the Discussion section with a paragraph that starts with the phrase, "In conclusion …." Or, "In summary …." This gives me the opportunity to summarize the important findings one more time and to end the paper with a strong statement of the importance of the work and its implications.

Below are two examples, one in which the conclusions were given as a separate section from the Discussion, and the other in which it was part of the Discussion.

Conclusions

We found that urban children with asthma, especially those in families with low incomes, are more likely than children without asthma to use special education services. In addition, we found that asthmatic children enrolled in special education are more likely to have uncontrolled asthma marked by use of urgent care services and inadequate asthma management. Finally, we found that the relation between enrollment in special education and some aspects of asthma management is mediated by socioeconomic variables and participation in asthma management or education programs. Overall, our results suggest that inadequate asthma control may contribute to a greater risk of special education placements among urban, asthmatic children.

From: Stingone JA and Claudio L, 2006

In conclusion, our results add more evidence that air pollution has a deleterious effect on children's lung function. Decrements in PEF and FEV_1 were observed with previous 24-h average exposure to air pollution, as well as with 3 to 10 day average exposure and were associated mainly with PM_{10}, NO_2, and O_3. Even though allergic sensitized children tended to present larger decrements in the PEF measurements when exposure to O_3 and PM_{10} were considered, these decrements were not statistically different than the decrements of the non-allergic sensitized. Given that children are exposed to this air on a daily basis, this exposure can lead to a chronic inflammatory process that might impair their lung growth and further their lung function in adulthood.

From: Correia-Deur JEM, Claudio L, Takimoto Imazawa A, Eluf-Neto J, 2012

Writing the References

The references are the sources of much of the information that you are presenting in your paper. It is the list of **_WHO_** did the previous work on which the paper is based. The references section (also called *citations, bibliography* or *literature cited*) has several purposes, one of which is to give credit where credit is due.

Remember the impact factors that we talked about in Chapter 7? Well, those are based on the number of times a paper is cited in other papers such as the paper that you are writing right now. This section serves to acknowledge the work of investigators who labored on your topic before you did, and helps to reinforce the fact that your work builds on the accomplishments of others, as it should.

In addition to giving proper credit to your sources, the references section points readers to additional information on the same topic. For instance, readers may want to find out more about a specific method that you used in your study, which may be detailed in another publication.

References also serve to substantiate your statements, and lend credibility to your study by supporting them with other publications.

 There are five main reasons for including citations to previously published research in your paper:

1. To provide evidence that supports your statements.

2. To give credit to the researchers who conducted the work on which you are basing your own work.

3. To avoid plagiarism, i.e., the appropriation of the works of others as if it were your own.

4. To compare your work with that of others published in the literature.

5. To provide readers with additional sources of information.

Reviewing the literature: General guidelines

The bulk of your citations will be included in the Introduction and in the Discussion sections of the paper. A few may fall under the Materials and Methods section to refer to a previously published protocol.

Prior to selecting a research question and designing your research project, you probably thoroughly reviewed the existing literature on your topic. You probably did this to gain a solid understanding of the current scientific knowledge, frame your study question, choose appropriate research methods and build on previously published works.

Your ability to carefully review the literature is one of the most fundamental skills that you will have to learn as a researcher. I am sure that you have been making an effort to keep up with the literature in your field of work. It is part of what you do as a researcher. However, the process of properly citing the references on which you base your writing for a research paper is very different than the everyday process of keeping up with the literature in your field. It requires focused reading and an understanding of the literature for the intentional purpose of substantiating the statements you make in your research paper.

Citing papers for the Introduction section requires you to capture the background knowledge that led you to pursue your particular research project. The idea is that your manuscript will present your research within the context of the current state of the science. In contrast, papers cited in the Discussion are used to compare and contrast your work with that of others.

 Evaluating published research papers

As you gather the articles that will serve as the background for and comparison to your research results, here are some key questions to keep in mind:

- **Who funded the research?** This information can be found in the acknowledgements section and can point towards a potential conflict of interest that the author may have. For example, an article on the benefits of smoking tobacco, when funded by a cigarette manufacturer, presents a conflict of interest. However, conflicts of interest are not always that obvious, so more journals are now requesting that authors specifically disclose potential conflicts of interest. If you choose to cite papers that represent a potential conflict of interest, make sure to point that out in your description of your citation.

- **Who are the authors?** Is the research team well recognized in the field? Have they produced other research studies that have advanced the topic in the past? Are they known for impartial research?

- **Do the research results match the concluding statements made in the abstract and elsewhere?** Are the results statistically strong enough to support the conclusions being stated, or are they based on weak data with low numbers of observations?

- **Is this a reputable journal?** Is the journal read widely among experts? What impact does this journal have in the field? Who are the people on the editorial board? Does it have a high impact factor in the field?

- **Is this a generalizable result?** Can the results be applied in a broader context, or is it a regional or special situation that may not hold true in other populations or may not be replicable?

Referencing: Accessing published literature

Medical journals are now available online, many through open access or through institutional subscriptions paid by your medical library. Most scientific journals are listed by the National Library of Medicine in the PubMed service and/or other similar indexing services. If you work in a medical research institution, you likely have access to one or various indexing systems through your intranet. If you do, then you should access PubMed through your intranet in order to get direct access to abstracts and the journals for which your library has subscriptions.

If you are not affiliated with a medical research center, or if your institution does not provide online access to an electronic medical library, then you can access PubMed directly through the internet. When you access PubMed directly through the internet, you can access the abstracts only. Unfortunately, you will not have direct access to the full journals unless they are "open access" journals. Open access journals are free of charge to readers. In this case, the publications are either paid for by the author or a government agency or professional society.

Another alternative way of accessing biomedical journals is to become a member of a research network. One research network that is growing in popularity is called ResearchGate. ResearchGate allows its members to post a repository of their own published and unpublished research as part of their profiles, which readers can access by downloading directly from their profile or requesting to receive a copy.

Yet another way to access published medical articles is to request them from the corresponding author directly. This will get you a free copy of the paper, but will not give you access to the journal where it was published. You can find the corresponding author's information through the abstracts that are published in PubMed, which include author information. When you click to expand that section, it will give you the institutional affiliation of the authors and the email address of the corresponding author who you can contact to request a copy of the paper or to ask any questions. (If you click on the individual names of the authors in the PubMed abstract, you will see other publications from those authors as well).

To cite or not to cite

It can be difficult to determine which statements need to be referenced. In general, any text or statement based on specific original works, whether it is the works by other authors or works by your own team, requires a reference.

Statements considered to be general or common knowledge do not require a reference. For instance, you can make the general statement, "Asthma is a common chronic disease among children." This statement is general knowledge and does not need to include a citation.

However, the statement, "The prevalence of asthma among children in New York was found to be 5.9%", needs a reference, because this is not considered common knowledge, and it is a specific finding reported in a particular publication.

Here is another example:

Reference needed:

Example: Heart attacks were the third leading cause of deaths in the United States in 2012.

Reference not needed:

Example: Heart disease is a major health concern in the United States.

The accidental plagiarist

Avoid plagiarism at all costs. This is partly why I think it is important to write with the source literature at hand. In my experience, most students commit plagiarism out of laziness—not out of malice. They know many of the facts that they need to include in their paper, but they don't remember where they read it. If they don't know where they read it, they can't cite the source. Some writers copy and paste information directly from a paper, and think that just because they included the reference that it is not plagiarism. Both are.

There are several common mistakes people make that constitute plagiarism. Some are:

No citation: To include information from other papers without crediting the source is plagiarism. Plagiarism is the appropriation of ideas from others into your own work. When in doubt, always cite the source. It is better to be accused of overzealous referencing than of plagiarism.

Copy/paste: Another common mistake is to copy and paste passages from other papers. Even if you include the citation, including exact words from another paper is not acceptable. The correct way to use your source literature is to read it, understand it, and paraphrase the important thoughts that you want to convey from that source.

Occasionally, the original author said it best, and you may decide to use a short direct quote. If you feel that you must include a sentence verbatim, then you must **use quotation marks** and a reference.

Self-plagiarism: Yes, there is such a thing as self-plagiarism. I previously suggested that you use your own previously written materials, such as sections from grant proposals, for the purposes of publishing in research papers. However, **if any part of your work has been previously published, it cannot be used again in another publication.**

Most journals will require that you relinquish your copyright for the material to them as a condition of publication. Therefore, once the material is published by that particular journal, you no longer hold the copyright. You can ask permission from the journal to reuse the material, or you can rephrase the writing and adapt it for your next paper.

As you gain experience publishing research papers, you will become more comfortable making these types of determinations. Soon, it will be second nature to know when to cite, when not to cite, when to quote, and when not to quote. Part of this process is getting well versed in your field—well-versed enough to be able to differentiate between what is a well-known fact and what needs to be referenced.

Other skills you will develop over time is determining which important references you'll need to cite for certain statements, who the authors are who typically publish certain types of studies in your field, and what the most important facts are that your readers need to know in order to get a good understanding of your paper. Gaining this mastery will significantly improve your writing skills.

As is true for every kind of writing, reading the kinds of publications that you would want to publish yourself will significantly improve your own writing.

> *To use your reference material, read the papers to be used for the section of the outline that you intend to write, take a moment to understand the concepts, and then write the information for your paper in your own words. If you copy statements from another paper, use quotation marks.*

Organize your references

If you have created a good outline, selecting and organizing your references will be fairly simple. Here are the steps creating a reference list for your paper:

1. Using your outline, determine the main subjects of each heading and subheading.

2. Use these main subjects from the headings and subheadings to conduct searches of the literature. PubMed is the most common and most comprehensive search engine and repository for conducting such searches.

3. Read the titles and abstracts of the papers you find. Determine which studies are most relevant to your paper. Also determine the relative validity of each paper (using the steps outlined above in *Evaluating Published Research Papers*).

4. Place the selected articles in the corresponding heading/subheading file folders (electronic or paper folders).

5. Have the appropriate folder containing the selected studies available when you sit down to write each section and subsection (typically a paragraph or two).

6. Read in depth the set of articles that pertain to the section that you intend to write. In each article, mark the sections, statements or facts that are most important for your paper. Make scribbles and notes on the articles to help you focus on the important parts of each article.

7. Write your text in your own words. Incorporate the citations as you write. Each paragraph that you write should be properly cited before you move onto the next. Citing your statements as you go will ensure that everything you say is fully backed by the evidence in the literature.

Format your citations

Whether you use a citation management program or enter your references by hand, you need to be conscious of the citation style required by the journal in which you intend to publish. The journal will provide detailed instructions about the citation style they require. This information is found in the Instructions for Authors, which should be in your files. You must follow these instructions exactly as given, carefully following all specified citation style requirements.

Most scientific journals require the Council for Science Editors (CSE) style citations. You can see more about their work at http://www.councilscienceeditors.org. The CSE has three variations for citations, as described below. While most journals require an established citation style such as CSE, some may provide additional instructions or citation requirements that supersede the CSE style. You will need to pay very close attention to information provided in the Instructions for Authors and follow those instructions exactly to the letter.

Regardless of which CSE format you use, you must include in-text citations. In-text citations are notes included in the text itself, immediately following or next to the information being cited. What varies among the three CSE style formats is how this information is displayed in the text. The three CSE formats are as follows:

- **Citation-Sequence Format**: Calls for a sequential superscript number (or a number in parentheses) at the end of the information credited to a source. The first referenced source appearing in your article will be numbered 1, the second will be numbered 2, and so on.

The same number will be used for that source in subsequent citations. For the reference list, sources are numbered and listed in numerical order (in the order in which they appear in the text).

- **Citation-Name Format**: This also uses superscript numbers (or numbers in parentheses) to attribute information in the text to a source. For this format, however, the reference list is created first, listing sources in alphabetical order by the first author's last name. Then, the references are numbered, and the appropriate number is used for in-text citations. The result will be that the reference numbers in the text will not be in numerical order.

- **Name-Year Format**: The names of authors and the year of publication of each reference are listed in parentheses in the text immediately after the information attributed to that source. In this style, the last name of the first author is included in the text in parenthesis. If there are more than two authors, the author's name is followed by the words "*et al*". If there are only two authors in the reference, the last names of both authors with the word "and" between them are included in the citation. After the names (or "et al"), there will be a comma and the year of publication. The reference list is organized alphabetically by the first author's last name without numbers.

Before you submit your article, it is your responsibility to make sure each statement is attributed to the correct source and that all citations and references are in the correct format specific to that journal. Using the right citation style from the very beginning will save you (and the editors) time and headache.

There are computer programs that help in managing citations and creating reference lists. Some of them let you input the reference directly from PubMed (so there is no need to retype it). You can then create your own database that includes all the references that you intend to use for your paper. Programs such as *Reference Manager, Endnote, Google Scholar and RefWorks* can be used to manage all or part of these tedious tasks.

There are several advantages to using a reference management program:

- You can create a database of references that you can reuse for different papers or grant proposals.

- When you edit your writing, the in-text citations and the reference list are automatically reformatted. This is especially useful when you move, add or delete cited sentences within your draft, as the citation will be anchored to the text and will be renumbered automatically.

- The reference list can be automatically formatted to the specific guidelines required by the journal.

Of course, there is a learning curve involved with any new computer program, but over the course of writing a few papers, this is time well spent, especially if you end up using some of the same references over and over again for future articles. If you decide that a reference program is right for you, simply choose the program that is easiest for you to use and that is most compatible with any software that your collaborators may use.

Alternatively, MS Word comes with a citation or endnote feature that can be used without having to buy another software program. Although somewhat limited in its functions, it has most of the basic features you need to create your bibliography. You can create a master database of references, insert citations into the text, format them and generally accomplish most other functions.

To insert citations and references in your text using MS Word, do the following:

1. Go to the References tab on the navigation ribbon.

2. Click Insert citation. If this is a new reference, it will take you to a form where you will be able to input all your reference data (authors, title, year of publication, etc.). One by one, you will create your database of references. The information will be available for your use in the future for the purposes of writing this and future articles.

3. MS Word will use this database of information to create a reference list. After you select the appropriate style from the References tab, MS Word will automatically put the information in the correct order and punctuate the list correctly according to your chosen style.

4. Be sure to verify that MS Word has correctly formatted and displayed each reference entry. It is your responsibility to verify that all information is accurate and conforms to the journal's requirements.

Although Word also has a Placeholder function within the Insert Citation command, I would discourage you from using it. Assuming you have the relevant literature on hand as you write, there is no valid reason why you would not enter the information in as you go, or at least after writing each paragraph. Citing your writing as you go is the best way to ensure efficiency and accuracy in your references.

As you grow your reference database, this process will become easier, more fluid and more intuitive.

Examples of in-text citations:

Other studies show that the rates of asthma among Latinos are three times the national average, while the rates for African-Americans are twice that level. [1,2]

In the example above, both sources provide the same information. If the two pieces of information were derived from two different published articles, then they should be listed as follows:

Other studies show that the rates of asthma for Latinos are three times the national average, [1] *while the rates for African-Americans is twice that level.* [2]

Another way to include in-text citations is to mention the name of the first author in the sentence. For example:

As Claudio and colleagues have shown, [1] *the rates of asthma for Latinos are three times the national average, while Stingone et al showed that the rates for African-American is twice that level.* [2]

Write the abstract

Some of you may already have an abstract that you created for a conference presentation. But before you skip this section, please note that your abstract needs to be reviewed after your article is complete. Only after the text of the full paper is complete can you be sure that your abstract perfectly reflects what you have written in your final manuscript.

The abstract is probably the most important part of your article. The purpose of the abstract is to concisely and accurately summarize the content of the entire paper, giving the reader a complete idea of what is presented in the paper and its conclusions. The abstract should convey the essence of the paper in very few words.

Why is the abstract so important? Today's journals publish an enormous number of journal articles—more than most people can read. For this reason, electronic services such as PubMed make article abstracts easily searchable and freely available. This feature exists because the abstracts are what many scientists read in order to keep up with the literature—just the abstracts. Most scientists only read full text of papers when the paper, as evidenced by the abstract, is particularly relevant to their work, it is work that they intend to cite or it is a paper that they intend to critique. Other than that, most people just read the titles and the abstracts.

Because the abstract is often the only thing many people will read (provided they find the title interesting), your abstract must accurately represent your paper. It also must be concise, well written, and able to hold the attention of the intended audience.

Because of the increased importance of the abstract, some journals require a *structured abstract* to ensure that all authors provide the important information in an organized and consistent format. Structured abstracts have subheadings that correspond roughly to each main heading in the article. For example, a structured abstract may include subheadings such as Background, Objective, Design and Setting, Participants, Main Outcome Measures, Results and Conclusions. Each of the structured abstract subsections should summarize each article section in one to four sentences.

Your ability to synthesize your work in brief and concise bites will help you immensely as you become a well-published scientist. Writing a great abstract is in itself and art and a science.

The word count limits for abstracts, whether structured or unstructured, should be taken as very strict limits that should never be exceeded. I know it can seem impossible to condense your entire article into a 200- to 500-word summary. But think of it as your elevator pitch. You only have a very short window of opportunity to grab the readers' attention. The title and the abstract ARE your opportunity to spread your message as broadly as possible. Make it count.

One way to make the process of writing your abstract easier is to initially write the abstract without adhering to the word count. After this step is complete, cut it down until it fits the journal's requirements. This allows you to see all of the information at once and determine which key pieces of information should remain in the final version. Many trainees get bogged down by the word-count limitation. If you find it difficult to write your abstract, follow the following steps.

Steps for writing an abstract

1. If your chosen journal requires a structured abstract, write out the headings they provide onto a blank sheet of paper. If they require an unstructured abstract, write the headings of each section of your paper: Introduction, Materials and Methods, Results, Discussion, Conclusions.

2. Go over each of the sections of your paper. Highlight the most important 1-4 sentences of each of the sections. Look for sentences or phrases that capture the essence of what your work is about.

3. Cut and paste those sentences onto the sheet of paper you previously created with the appropriate headings.

4. Rework and edit the sentences you chose. Rephrase them, combine them and narrow them down to the most important. Take out words that are not needed. See how you can say the same thing with fewer words.

5. Check the word count and make sure that you have not gone over the limit.

6. If the journal requires an unstructured abstract, take out the headings. Make sure to fix the transitions between sections so that the writing flows with ease.

Once you have the abstract down to the word limit required, carefully review the abstract to make sure that it adequately reflects the substance of your article.

 Remember, a good abstract should state the salient points of the paper, and will give the reader a very good idea of what is contained in the paper. The abstract should give the complete plot, and not leave much to the imagination. It is not a teaser for a mystery novel; it is a true summary of the complete paper. When it comes to abstracts for scientific papers, spoiler alerts do not apply. Your intention should be to provide the reader with all important information about your paper.

Example of a structured abstract found in PubMed:

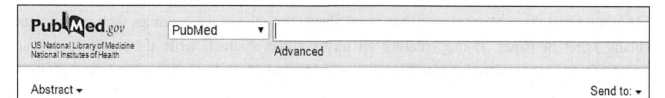

Abstract ▾   Send to: ▾

Contemp Clin Trials. 2012 Nov;33(6):1197-205. doi: 10.1016/j.cct.2012.07.014. Epub 2012 Aug 4.

Socioeconomic determinants associated with willingness to participate in medical research among a diverse population.

Svensson K[1], Ramírez OF, Peres F, Barnett M, Claudio L.

⊕ Author information

Abstract

INTRODUCTION: Although it is federally-mandated that racial/ethnic minorities be included in research studies, recruiting diverse populations remains a challenge. This is particularly difficult when research involves children. The purpose of this study was to assess attitudes and beliefs toward medical research among a racially and socioeconomically diverse population of parents of school children.

METHODS: A cross-sectional parent-report survey was conducted in New York City public elementary schools using stratified random selection to obtain a diverse population. Fear of medical research and likelihood to participate in medical research were assessed using a validated questionnaire. Differences in fear/likelihood to participate in research across race/ethnicity and socioeconomic characteristics were evaluated.

RESULTS: In general, parents were afraid of their child "being treated as a guinea pig", but were willing to allow their child to participate in research if asked by their own doctor. Factors associated with a lower score on fear toward research were; primary language other than English (OR=0.59), access to an interpreter (OR=0.73) and access to medical service within a day (OR=0.51). Latinos had the highest fear score (OR=1.87) compared to Whites. Asians were the ethnic group most likely to participate in research (OR=1.71). Low education level (OR=2.18) and public health insurance (OR=1.37) were associated with a higher score for likelihood of allowing one's child to participate in medical research.

CONCLUSION: Minority parents reported more fear of allowing their children to participate in medical research, but were as likely to consent their children's participation, especially if asked by their own physician.

PMID: 22885788 [PubMed - indexed for MEDLINE] PMCID: PMC3515640 Free PMC Article

Example of an unstructured abstract:

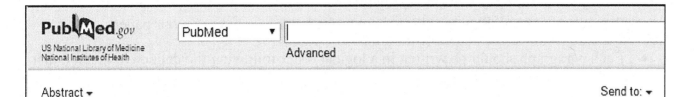

Abstract ▾

Send to: ▾

J Urban Health. 2010 Mar;87(2):211-24. doi: 10.1007/s11524-009-9404-1. Epub 2010 Jan 9.

The role of housing type and housing quality in urban children with asthma.

Northridge J[1], Ramirez OF, Stingone JA, Claudio L.

⊕ **Author information**

Abstract

The goal of this study was to assess the relationship between type and quality of housing and childhood asthma in an urban community with a wide gradient of racial/ethnic, socioeconomic, and housing characteristics. A parent-report questionnaire was distributed in 26 randomly selected New York City public elementary schools. Type of housing was categorized using the participants' addresses and the Building Information System, a publicly-accessible database from the New York City Department of Buildings. Type of housing was associated with childhood asthma with the highest prevalence of asthma found in public housing (21.8%). Residents of all types of private housing had lower odds of asthma than children living in public housing. After adjusting for individual- and community-level demographic and economic factors, the relationship between housing type and childhood asthma persisted, with residents of private family homes having the lowest odds of current asthma when compared to residents of public housing (odds ratio: 0.51; 95% confidence interval, 0.22, 1.21). Factors associated with housing quality explain some of the clustering of asthma in public housing. For example, the majority (68.7%) of public housing residents reported the presence of cockroaches, compared to 21% of residents of private houses. Reported cockroaches, rats, and water leaks were also independently associated with current asthma. These findings suggest differential exposure and asthma risk by urban housing type. Interventions aimed at reducing these disparities should consider multiple aspects of the home environment, especially those that are not directly controlled by residents.

PMID: 20063071 [PubMed - indexed for MEDLINE] PMCID: PMC2845835   Free PMC Article

 As a rule of thumb, I write all abstracts in a structured format, whether or not a journal requires it. This serves as a guide to ensure that all important aspects of the paper are included. If the journal does not require structured abstracts, I remove the subheadings before submitting.

Points to remember from Chapter 9

- Each journal has very specific instructions for authors. You must print them out and have them close at hand. Plan to follow them to the letter as you write your paper.

- Each paragraph should be written in a logical order following the deductive method that systematically organizes the writing from general to more specific. The paper should be organized in this way at the micro level (at the level of the paragraphs) as well as at the macro level (each section of the paper).

- Each section of a research paper aims to answer a specific question.

  - Title – A descriptive label that allows potential readers to decide quickly whether they should invest time in reading the paper.

  - Abstract – A comprehensive summary of the full paper.

  - Introduction – Explains WHY the study was conducted.

  - Materials and Methods – Details the HOW the study was done.

  - Results – Recounts WHAT was discovered.

  - Discussion – Answers the question of: SO WHAT? Explains what is important about the paper and compares the results to ones obtained by others.

  - References – The list of WHO is cited in the paper. The literature on which the study was built.

- Plagiarism is a serious mistake. Avoid by citing your sources correctly.

- The abstract is a very important part of your paper because most people will only read the abstract. Ensure that it summarizes the full paper. Even if the journal does not require a structured abstract, use the headings of your paper to extract the most important messages from each section.

Additional Resources

The Elements of Style by William Strunk, Jr. 2015 – The original version of this book, coauthored by E.B. White, is one on the most used references for grammar in the English language.

Exercise 9a: *The why, the how, the what and the so what?*

Answer these questions in concise and direct terms. Pretend that a very smart reporter is asking you the questions for a popular science magazine. Be concise and to the point, but be informative.

Example: From Deierlein AL, Peat K, Claudio L, 2014:
WHY did you conduct this study?

> *The food environment is very influential in shaping children's diets, and may contribute to obesity. Restaurant meals are a significant proportion of children's diets. Half of US children consume fast food. Our objective was to evaluate if popular restaurants have made changes in children's menus.*

HOW did you conduct this research?

> - *Analyzed data for restaurant chains ranked in the top 50 in US sales.*
> - *Nutritional data from menus was entered into a database.*
> - *Permutations of main and side dishes were created from the database.*
> - *Calculated the percent of main and side dishes that exceeded federal recommendations for calories from fat and sodium.*
> - *Mean nutrient content of added, removed and unchanged menu items were compared between 2010 and 2014.*

WHAT did you find?

> - *Nutrient content of main dishes did not change between 2010 and 2014.*
> - *One-third of main dishes at fast-food restaurant chains exceeded Dietary Guidelines for sodium, fat, and saturated fat in 2014.*
> - *Improvements in nutrient content were observed for side dishes.*

SO, WHAT is important about this study?

> - *The majority of menu items—especially main dishes—available to children still contain high amounts of calories, fat, saturated fat, and sodium.*
> - *Efforts must be made by the restaurant industry and policy makers to improve the nutritional content of children's menu items at restaurant chains to align with the Dietary Guidelines for Americans.*
> - *Additional efforts are necessary to help parents and children make informed choices when ordering at restaurant chains.*

Exercise 9b: The why, the how, the what and the so what?

Answer these questions in concise and direct terms. Pretend that a very smart reporter is asking you the questions for a popular science magazine. Be concise and to the point, but be informative.

WHY did you conduct this study?

HOW did you conduct this research?

WHAT did you find?

SO, WHAT is important about this study?

You may go to www.drluzclaudio.com and download the forms for the following exercises, which you will be able to customize to fill in.

Chapter 10: Collaborating with Other Researchers

"Always remember that you are absolutely unique. Just like everyone else."
— Margaret Mead, American anthropologist, author and speaker

No scientist works alone. Throughout your career you will collaborate with a number of other scientists when conducting your research, whether as a student, postdoctoral fellow or lab director.

While you are a fledgling student, you are under the guidance and supervision of a mentor who guides you and teaches you the ways and means of conducting research. Mentors come in all styles, shapes, and forms. Some are very hands-on, guiding you at every step, including during the writing process. Others are hands-off, allowing you to grow and learn at your own pace. Most are in-between the two extremes.

Each kind of mentor expects different levels of independence from their mentees during the research process and the writing process. If you are a student or postdoctoral fellow, check with your mentor to see if they will allow you to write first drafts of research papers, and ask about the level of independence they expect from you in that process.

Scientists with more experience will have collaborators at different levels contributing to their research papers. Some research collaborators will be technicians and students with limited experience, but whose contributions to the research are still important. Other collaborators may be senior scientists or peers that contribute intellectually and fundamentally to the study design. These collaborations are important for the research and data collection phases, and continue to be important during the writing process.

The senior scientist is usually the person who obtained the main funding or grant for the study (usually the person whose name is on the door of the lab and is ultimately responsible for the team). She or he is usually the principal investigator responsible for the funding of the research and is a faculty member at the research institution if it is an academic setting. This person is responsible for the work, obtains funding for continued support of the research, provides progress reports to the funding agency, makes fiscal decisions, and is ultimately responsible for the conduct and integrity of the research project.

The key to success in coordinating a team of authors for your paper is to have open communication throughout the process. Ideally, from the beginning of the research project, all of the authors should agree on the roles each will play in the writing and editing processes. I say "ideally" because often the authorship question is not addressed until a paper is drafted and is about to be submitted. Addressing issues of authorship can be a painful process, but it does not have to be. First, let's discuss the different ways in which the responsibility of writing a paper may be split among the potential coauthors.

How to write a paper with a research team

There are a number of different ways in which groups of scientists collaboratively write a manuscript. Some teams divide the outline and assign each member of the research group a section or sections to write. Other teams have only the senior scientist write and submit all papers, and he/she determines the persons who will be included as coauthors.

In my opinion, it is usually not a good idea to divide the task of writing a paper by having each author write a different section. This is because each person will have a different writing style, and even if they follow the same outline, they will have different perspectives on the data and on what is important. The end result of writing by committee tends to be disjointed, takes much longer to complete, requires careful coordination and can lead to strained relationships.

That being said, it is sometimes necessary to write as a group, especially when the paper is complex and has different parts that were done by different people, maybe with different disciplines or areas of expertise. Either way, it is important to note that ALL contributing scientists are responsible for the WHOLE paper. Every contributor must be completely aware of and understand every section of the manuscript, including the sections that they did not write themselves.

The steps I recommend that you follow when you are writing a paper collaboratively with your coauthors are in the sections below.

Steps to writing a first draft with a group of cowriters

If you want to divide the task of writing the paper among some or all of your coauthors, it will be imperative that everyone is, literally, on the same page. That page, is of course, the outline.

Having everyone working off the same outline will ensure that all authors agree on the main goals and content of the paper and that the writing is as cohesive as possible in spite of multiple writing styles and points of view. The steps that I recommend for this style of collaboration are:

1. **Take charge** – someone has to lead the group. Let that be you. It is a great experience as you move towards becoming an independent scientist, if you are not one already. Become the leader and expect high standards from yourself and each member of the group.

2. **Draft the outline** – The outline will serve as a way to organize everyone's writing.

3. **Present the outline to the group in person** – Whether you are physically together or talking through video conference, it is important for the outline to be initially discussed in person by everyone who may coauthor the paper. Convene a meeting and use the outline as the agenda. Go point by point on each of the topics and subtopics outlined. Edit the outline as you discuss it in person at this meeting and make sure that each coauthor agrees, at least in general terms, on the content of each of the topics and subtopics.

4. **Present options for appropriate journals to the group** – As explained in Chapter 7, having a good idea from the start about what journal you are targeting will facilitate the writing process. Armed with this knowledge, you can gear the writing to the style required by the journal and can focus on the relevant points for that particular readership. Ideally, you can decide on the target journal during the first authors' meeting. Distribute the Instructions for Authors for each journal option that you are considering to all coauthors prior to the meeting so that a final decision on the journal can be made at this meeting.

5. **Divide the work** – Next to each topic and subtopic of the outline, write the name of each coauthor responsible for writing it. The amount of writing that each of you commits to doing does not need to be equitable. Simply determine who is the best person for each job based on:

   a. the work they did during the research process,

   b. their access to the information needed to write each section,

   c. their availability, and

   d. their knowledge or expertise on the topic.

   Ideally, try to have the same coauthor write longer stretches of text rather than having authors alternate writing the shorter sections.

6. **Set deadlines** – Do not end the meeting without having everyone look at their calendar and committing to firm deadlines for completing their sections. Deadlines should be mutually agreed upon and be taken seriously by all coauthors involved.

7. **Decide on a collaboration system** – There are a number of web-based tools that will facilitate collaboration on a manuscript by multiple authors in real time. Dropbox and Googledocs are two of the most well-known, but there are others. Some institutions also have internal systems for sharing files. Check with your coauthors to see what tool they want to use. The goal is to have a live manuscript that automatically updates as authors enter their contributions. Avoid emailing each other the sections of the manuscript. This is a terribly inefficient way to collaborate in your writing.

8. **Use the outline as a template** – Post the outline on the collaboration system you decide to use. Use it as a template for having the collaborators insert their writing. You may include the names of each of the coauthors who committed to write each section of the outline and the deadline that they agreed upon for completing their writing as a more detailed reminder for the group.

9. **Revise drafts**– Once coauthors have submitted their draft sections by their respective deadlines, the lead author should take on the task of editing the full paper. This should be done with an eye for consistency. Look to create a cohesive whole. Make sure that the same terms are used throughout the paper. Make sure the paper has the same tone throughout, and that the same conclusions are emphasized. Clarify contradictory statements. Add transition statements between sections and ensure there is a good flow between sections written by different coauthors.

10. **Arrive at consensus** – The paper is ready to be submitted when all authors agree that it is ready. Avoid arguments with coauthors by establishing deadlines for writing, editing and submitting. The group should try to avoid working on the paper via an open-ended system in which coauthors can edit and re-edit forever. Be firm on the editing schedule, or the paper will never be submitted. Once everyone has agreed to submit the paper, have them sign the submission statement form that is required by the journal. In it, all coauthors must agree on the content of the paper and their respective contributions.

Writing the first draft yourself

I believe that every young scientist should prepare to become an author. And the only way to become an author is by writing. Part of my mentoring duties includes mentoring students on writing. As such, I make it a priority to focus on the process of putting research into words.

In some research teams, however, the senior scientist writes the research papers. The person who takes responsibility for being the primary writer of the paper should have firsthand knowledge of the research that was conducted, and should have access to all the data—even the raw data—for all parts of the study.

If you are that person, it is important for you to polish your leadership skills and take control of the writing in a way that is respectful of all the coauthors, which will allow them to have enough input on the final product. The steps that I recommend for writing a first draft of a paper for a research group are:

1. **Write your title and outline** – As explained throughout this book, the outline should be comprehensive and contain all topics and subtopics that will appear in the final paper. Be as clear as possible in your outline. Avoid using shorthand or terms that only you understand, because you will need to share this outline with your coauthors.

2. **Collect Instructions for Authors for three potential journals** – Follow the instructions provided in Chapter 7.

3. **Send the draft Title, Outline Data Tables/Figures and Instructions for Authors for the three journal choices to the other collaborators** – If you have presented the work at a conference and have an abstract, send that as well. Ask for a meeting to discuss writing the work for publication.

4. **Meet with your coauthors** – During this meeting, go over all of the figures, tables, graphs and any other representation of the Results that will be included in the paper. Remove all that will not be included in this particular paper. Agree on the interpretation of the results and how they will be represented in the paper. Agree on a deadline by which you expect to have the first draft completed.

5. **Follow the instructions in this book (if you are taking our Write Science Now course, follow the assignments)** – Organize yourself in order to meet the deadline that you set with your coauthors.

6. **Share the draft** –There are two possibilities here: One is that you draft the entire paper and only share it with your coauthors once it has all the sections. The other possibility is that you share each draft section as you complete them. Whichever approach you use to sharing your drafts mainly depends on your experience and ability to write a research paper. I personally prefer to write the whole thing myself, and then ask for edits and comments from my coauthors. However, if too much time will pass before you can complete the whole draft, then you should share the sections as you complete them.

7. **Request input** – As you write, you may encounter sections on which you have questions or comments for your coauthors. Highlight those sections in the manuscript and enter your specific question as a "Comment". Put the draft manuscript in a sharable document (using Googledocs, Dropbox or other) and invite your coauthors to provide edits and feedback to you by a specific deadline. You may want to have your coauthors enter their edits using the "Track Changes" function in Word. Whether you accept all suggested changes or not, make sure to always acknowledge the suggestion in the comments.

8. **Create new draft** – Considering all coauthors' comments, create a second draft, and circulate for a second round of comments by a certain deadline. Each time you issue a new draft, request a shorter and shorter turnaround time for submitting comments and edits from your coauthors. For instance, give your coauthors one month after the first draft to submit edits, then three weeks after the second draft, two weeks after the third, etc. This will get you closer to getting the paper ready for submission rather than producing endless drafts in a vicious cycle.

9. **Resolve disagreements in person** – In the event that one or more coauthors are chronically late in submitting revisions to the drafts or do not agree with some important areas of the paper, talk with them in person or by phone to discuss the issue. This is important to resolving any issues and to moving the paper along.

10. **Set a submission deadline** – Intend to submit the paper by this deadline unless there is strong opposition from a coauthor. If that is the case, you may want to convene a meeting to see how the objection may be resolved within the group.

During the process of writing with collaborators, it is important to remember that your collaborators' comments on your writing should be taken as constructive criticism meant to improve the overall manuscript, and not as personal attacks on your writing abilities. Everyone's goal should be to submit a great paper that will be accepted for publication in a highly reputable journal. Even when everyone has the same goal in mind, sometimes disagreements may occur. For example, someone may disagree over the most appropriate way to present results or which journal to choose. These occurrences are always best handled with open and respectful communication.

As a junior investigator, please keep in mind that the more seasoned collaborators can provide good advice based on their previous experience in preparing manuscripts for publication. That does not mean you should always defer to their suggestions; however, you should consider every recommendation with an open mind. If you disagree with a recommendation, it is important to clearly and respectfully state why you do not think it would improve the manuscript, rather than just discarding it is as a bad idea. Most likely, you will work with your collaborators again in the future, so it is in the best interest of your career to forge positive relationships during this process.

Determining authorship

In my view, the person who writes the first draft should also be the first author listed, even if the person is relatively junior—assuming that the draft is fairly good, of course.

Traditionally, the last author placement is occupied by the senior investigator of the study. This is usually the principal investigator of the grant supporting the project, or the laboratory leader. This person may not have conducted the experiments hands-on, but may have conceived of the concepts, developed the study design, obtained the funding or approved the experimental methods. This is the person ultimately responsible for the report.

This senior investigator is often the person responsible for communication with the journal and its editors, and is often listed as the "corresponding author" or "To whom correspondence should be addressed" in the title page of the manuscript. All correspondence regarding the paper, including the reviewer comments and publication decisions, will be sent directly and only to the corresponding author.

Other authors can be added in between the first and last author in an order that reflects their contributions to the paper. The names and order of authorship can be a subject of contention among otherwise very collegial research collaborators. Don't let that happen to you. Authorship should be decided during your initial outline discussion meeting. The principal investigator should take responsibility for determining authorship and the order of the authors. Fairness should be your guide in trying to reflect the contributions of your colleagues.

One common trap many investigators fall into when determining authorship is the attempt to include everyone and anyone who had anything to do with the paper, or anyone who was present in the lab or office where the research was conducted. This is a mistake. Authors should be those and only those persons who contributed significantly to the completion of the research and the paper. Period.

Significant contributors include those who:

- Developed the concept and study design of the research conducted,

- Provided novel scholarly interpretation of results, added a section to the paper or suggested a research approach.

- Conducted the actual experiments, collected and/or analyzed the data, (however, note here that persons who collect data under exact directions of a supervisor may not necessarily be included as coauthors. Examples are surveyors, interviewers or technicians).

Of course, there may be other people whose contributions were important and without whom the paper would not have been completed. However, if they don't fall within the categories listed above, they should not be listed as authors. These contributors should be recognized in the acknowledgements section of your paper.

Here are some examples of contributors who should be acknowledged (but not listed as authors):

- Students who contributed to the paper, other than intellectual contributors. This may include junior summer students who collected surveys or entered values into a database.

- Technicians and research assistants who conduct work exactly as instructed by a researcher.

- Secretarial staff who type or proofread the paper.

- Colleagues—even senior colleagues—who read the paper and gave you editorial suggestions or comments related to the style of the paper.

The exercise following provides a hypothetical example for determining authorship.

CONSIDER THIS SCENARIO ...

You are the principal investigator in a grant that aims to find which factors contribute to diabetes in an urban population.

You and your postdoctoral fellow design a screening tool that predicts diabetes in adults. In consultation with a departmental biostatistician, you determine that you will need to screen 1,000 subjects in order to have enough statistical power.

The postdoctoral fellow meets with the research assistant of your office and asks her to call potential participants from an existing list of previously-consented patients. The research assistant is only able to recruit 55 people, because this list is outdated. The research assistant suggests at your weekly lab meeting that you try recruiting patients from the WW Community Center. You think this is a great idea and modify the protocol accordingly. You also decide to enlist the help of two of your smartest summer students to work with WW Community Center.

The recruitment is a success, and you present the preliminary results at the Annual Conference to Fight Diabetes. At the conference, Dr. Knowitall gives your postdoctoral fellow some helpful comments about how to present the data more clearly. The biostatistician finalizes the data analysis and the graphs for the paper. The postdoctoral fellow drafts the whole paper. Now you must determine authorship and acknowledgments.

ANSWER...

> <u>**Authors**</u>
>
> Postdoctoral fellow - first author
> Biostatistician - third author (at your discretion)
> Research Assistant - second author
> Principal Investigator (You) - last (senior) author
>
> <u>**Acknowledgments**</u>
>
> Summer students, listed individually (if no particular student participated in the study, then acknowledge the student program)
> Dr. Knowitall for her helpful insight
> WW Community Gym Managers (for their outreach to potential participants)

Acknowledge your contributors

The acknowledgement section is designed to credit the contributions of those who provided significant input into the conduct of the project or the paper itself, except for those who already appear as authors. Although the contributions may have been limited, they still are significant and should be recognized.

The acknowledgements section should state clearly who you are thanking and why, but should be limited to a single short paragraph. State what was the specific contribution that the individual or institution made to the research or the writing of the paper.

Some journals require you to include the funding source within the Acknowledgements section, while others require you to include the funding source in a separate section. Either way, the funding source should include the granting agency and grant number, if applicable.

When you report your accomplishments to that funder, you should mention that their support led to a research publication. Funders appreciate this acknowledgement of their support, and some require acknowledgement in every publication that stems from their funding.

For scientific studies, acknowledgement is also a matter of disclosure. For example, I might be skeptical of a cigarette company-funded article that presents the significant health benefits of smoking. While this is an extreme example, listing the funding source provides a mechanism with which readers can assess a possible conflict of interest of the authors/funders. Because the conflict of interest is such a potentially contentious issue, many journals are now requiring authors to disclose in their article any potential conflict of interest, as well as provide a signed statement regarding any actual or potential conflict of interest.

 Example of an acknowledgments section that includes funding sources:

Thanks to Dr. Soandso for providing the questionnaire used in this study, to Ms. Allthat for translating research materials into Spanish and to Student 1 and Student 2 from the Summer Scholars Program for serving as student interviewers. This work was supported by a grant from the NIHS (XS000020) and from the Fast Foundation (Grant 12345). Dr. White's work was also supported by a MARK Award for Minority Faculty (XS00000010).

Points to remember from Chapter 10

- When writing a paper with a writing team, make sure to take charge of the writing plan. Distribute the outline and ensure that everyone agrees who will write each section, as well as the deadline for submitting contributions to the group.

- When committing to write the first draft by yourself, make sure that all potential coauthors agree on the outline that you will follow and on the scope and interpretation of the results to be included in the article.

- Agree with coauthors on a web-based document sharing system that can accept edits from multiple contributors. Avoid emailing different versions of the paper to coauthors. All edits should be made within a central document that is accessible to all authors.

- Aim to determine authorship early in the writing process. Final authorship must be determined before the paper is sent in for publication. You may use an Authorship Determination Scoring Sheet if there are difficulties in determining authorship.

- All other contributors and funding sources should be mentioned in the Acknowledgements section.

Exercise 10a: Determining authorship

Discuss authorship with your collaborators before the paper is submitted. Here, I have adapted an authorship determination instrument. The instrument may be helpful in instances where there is disagreement regarding authorship. (Adapted from Winston, Jr. R.B. (1985) A suggested procedure for determining the order of authorship in research publications. Journal of Counseling and Development, 63, 515-518) Also at: http://www.apa.org

Example for paper: Peres F, Rodrigues KM, da Silva Peixoto Belo MS, Moreira JC, Claudio L. Design of risk communication strategies based on risk perception among farmers exposed to pesticides in Rio de Janeiro State, Brazil. Am J Ind Med. 2013 Jan; 56(1):77-89

Activity	Points	Method Used*	Contributor Score — Initials of each potential coauthor					
			PF	RK	SM	MJ	CL	KC
Conceptualizing research	50	Q	√			√		
Methods design	40	Q/T	√					
Data collection and preparation	40	Q/T	√	√	√			
Statistical analyses	20	Q		√	√			
Literature search	10	T					√	
Drafting of manuscripts First Draft	50	T	√					
Second Draft	30	T					√	
Redrafting (per page)	2	T				√		
Manuscript editing	10	T					√	√
Total score**			*180*	*60*	*60*	*52*	*50*	*10*

*Q – points based on qualitative criteria for assessing the amount of work

*T – points based on quantitative criteria such as time expended, total pages drafted

*Q/T – points assigned based on qualitative and quantitative criteria

** Anyone getting 50 points or more should be listed as an author. Contributors getting less than 50 points should be listed on the Acknowledgements.

Exercise 10b: Determining authorship

Discuss authorship with your collaborators before the paper is submitted. Here, I have adapted an authorship determination instrument. The instrument may be helpful in instances where there is disagreement regarding authorship. (Adapted from Winston, Jr. R.B. (1985) A suggested procedure for determining order of authorship in research publications. Journal of Counseling and Development, 63, 515-518) Also at: http://www.apa.org

AUTHORSHIP DETERMINATION SCORING SHEET

Activity	Points	Method Used*	Contributor Score Initials of each potential coauthor					
Conceptualizing research	50	Q						
Methods design	40	Q/T						
Data collection and preparation	40	Q/T						
Statistical analyses	20	Q						
Literature search	10	T						
Drafting of manuscripts First Draft	50	T						
Second Draft	30	T						
Redrafting (per page)	2	T						
Manuscript editing	10	T						
Total score**								

*Q – points assigned based on qualitative criteria for assessing the amount of work

*T – points assigned based on quantitative criteria such as time expended or total pages drafted

*Q/T – points assigned based on qualitative and quantitative criteria

** Anyone getting 50 points or more should be listed as an author. Contributors getting less than 50 points should be listed on the Acknowledgements.

> You may go to www.drluzclaudio.com and download the forms for the following exercises, which you will be able to customize to fill in.

Chapter 11: The Manuscript is Finished... Now What?

"It takes considerable knowledge just to realize the extent of your own ignorance."

— **Thomas Sowell, American economist, philosopher and author**

So, you've done everything right. You've collected solid, ground-breaking data. You have analyzed it. You have derived profound conclusions from it. You have produced a clear, readable paper closely following the Instructions for Authors of a journal that you have carefully selected. Now what?

 Now it is time to send your paper in for consideration to the journal's editor-in-chief. The paper should be submitted online on the journal's website. Once your paper is written, the process of submission can take just a few minutes depending on your experience and the journal's portal design.

Some journal portals require that you submit each section of the paper separately. Other portals allow you to submit the paper as a single pdf. Either way, once you register for the portal, it is relatively easy to follow the instructions for submitting your paper.

It is important to note that there are publishing companies that manage many journals under the same online portal. You must therefore be sure to send your article to the right journal within that portal. Other than that, you should find the process of actually submitting your paper quite easy.

Your paper must be accompanied by a cover letter. Many journals provide specific wording that must be included in the cover letter, which is directed to the editor-in-chief. If specific language is not given, you can use the sample cover letter below as a guide. Some journals require that all coauthors sign this letter, while other journals require a signature only for the corresponding author. Either way, follow the instructions and you will be fine.

Sample of a cover letter for submitting a paper

Dear Dr. (Enter name of Editor-in-Chief)

Enclosed is our manuscript entitled, "Breast cancer intervention program in Brooklyn, New York" by Drs. Me, Dr. Her and Dr. Other for your consideration in the *Journal of Many Things*.

The manuscript is not being considered for publication elsewhere. An abstract of this manuscript was previously presented at the Conference of New Findings in 2015 and published in its proceedings (Journal of New Findings, p. 24, 2015).

We would like to recommend the following reviewers:

Dr. James Doe – University of Elsewhere

Dr. Susan Notafriend – Another University

Dr. Pat Nevermet – Faraway Medical Center

Thank you for your consideration of this manuscript.

Sincerely,

Dr. Me & Dr. Her

Our City, Our State

Recommending reviewers for your paper

One of the main bottlenecks in the publication process is receiving the critique in a timely manner. Editors are very busy people, and reviewers are unpaid volunteers. Finding the right reviewers can greatly facilitate the process and can speed up the consideration of your paper for publication.

As such, many editors appreciate receiving suggestions from the authors regarding potential reviewers. Some journals may even ask for you to recommend reviewers. If so, it will be stated in the Instructions for Authors or there may be a form in the portal to enter your recommended reviewers.

Here are some issues that can delay the review once a paper has been submitted:

- The journal does not have any reviewers in your specific field in their roster

- It is a particularly busy time of year (e.g., holidays, grant deadlines, a time near a professional conference in your field)

- Your field is very narrow, novel or unique, so there are few available experts with the right type of expertise to review your paper

Do not be tempted to include names of people who are too closely connected to you, such as friends or competitors. Friends may feel conflicted about serving as reviewers. Most would state that they have a conflict of interest and would not accept the assignment to review your paper. This will delay your publication. Competitors may be tempted to give a negative review or intentionally delay the review process.

In recommending reviewers for your paper, choose people who are familiar with your field, but have a neutral view of your work. Your recommended reviewers should work at other institutions, not your own, and should not have any real or perceived conflicts of interest regarding the publication of your work.

Some ways in which you can find potential reviewers to recommend to the journal are:
- Talk to your coauthors and see if they have any ideas.

- Consider people who have approached you or commented on your work at professional conferences.

- Consider people whom you cite in your paper and who have published related works.

- Consider people who have taught courses or presented lectures in your field of work.

Journals are increasingly requesting reviewer recommendations as part of the submission, and you should be prepared to provide some names. So keep track of people who might serve as reviewers as you develop your work for publication.

Please note that your list of suggested reviewers may not be heeded. Even if those suggested reviewers are asked, they may not accept the invitation to review your paper. The editor-in-chief is under no obligation to request the review from the list of recommended reviewers that you provide.

Who's who in the journal

Editors-in-chief have the ultimate power over the final decision of whether a paper gets published in their journal. But journals also have an editorial board composed of additional editors who may handle subspecialties under the general topic of the journal or may cover certain kinds of papers or sections for the journal. These editors are usually well-recognized experts in their field who volunteer their valuable time to wade through dozens or perhaps hundreds of manuscript submissions each year. The editor-in-chief may rely on the editorial board for guidance on the scope of the works being published in the journal or may assign them to do the final review of particular papers. Go over the names listed in the editorial board to give you an idea of who might be assigned to review your paper.

Journals may also add guest editors from time to time. Guest editors are experts who are well recognized in a subspecialty related to the main topic of the journal invited by the editor-in-chief to serve as editor for a particular issue or edition of the journal that may focus on a subspecialty. Typically, these special issues of a journal tend to publish a "call for papers". This call for papers serves as an invitation to the readership to contribute papers for consideration in the special issue of the journal. There is usually a deadline for submission to a call for papers, as all the papers accepted under that special call will be published in the same edition of the journal.

Most likely, the editor-in-chief has the assistance of a managing editor who is in charge of receiving, logging, and sending the manuscripts out to reviewers and following up with reviewers and authors. Once the paper is reviewed and you receive and respond to the critiques, you will be communicating with this person to get the paper ready for publication.

After your manuscript arrives to the journal, the managing editor will scan it to see if it fits the theme and format of the journal. If it doesn't, it will be returned to you without further review. If it does, the managing editor will send it to the editor-in- chief (or sometimes another senior editor on the editorial board) who will list potential reviewers that the managing editor can send your manuscript to.

Usually, at least two reviewers are asked to provide comments. These comments will include details on the specific merits and shortcomings of the paper. If these two reviewers strongly disagree (one thinks the paper is publishable and the other says it's not), the editor-in-chief can do any of the following: a) send your paper to a third reviewer for a tiebreaker, b) determine that the manuscript is acceptable for publication after you answer the critiques, or c) determine that the manuscript is unacceptable for publication.

Who are these reviewers? Who are those peers who get to pass judgment on your work? They are people just like you. They may work in a similar area as you, so some of them may be your colleagues or competitors. They are unpaid volunteers who agree to serve as reviewers for the journal. They may have previously published a paper in that same journal. Or maybe they have published articles in similar areas of work as yours. You may never know who they are, because the comments are given to you anonymously. Peer reviewers are the faceless and powerful engine that drives the research publication structure.

The peer review process

When you submit a paper for consideration to a journal, it can feel like sending it into a black box. A mysterious process happens inside that box, and out comes a published paper. Let's try to take the mystery out of the review process.

The first thing that happens when you submit a paper is that the managing editor will check to see if the paper fits the journal's requirements for theme, language, word count limit and other basic requirements. If he/she determines that your submitted paper fits these criteria, then the paper will be sent to editor-in-chief or to one of the content editors in the editorial board. A determination is then made on which peers will review your paper.

Many journals remove the title page of submitted papers before sending them to peer reviewers. Conversely, they also remove the names of the reviewers from the critique that you will receive. This double-blind approach helps to ensure that works are evaluated on their individual merits, and not on reputation (or lack of one).

Again, peer reviewers are unpaid volunteers who agree to read papers for a particular journal and submit their comments and recommendations to the editor, who then sends the critiques to you. As you experience this process, you will find that most reviewers will offer generous insight, and spend a significant amount time and effort reading your manuscript in detail. In most cases, you will find that their comments are helpful and implementing their recommendations and suggestions will indeed improve the paper.

Don't be afraid to expose your work to peer review. It will improve the outcome. Don't take the critiques personally. Your goal is to receive the critiques impartially and objectively and decide which feedback comments, if heeded, will improve the paper.

Think of it this way: someone very knowledgeable took the time and effort to read your work in detail. That should give you some comfort in the process.

If your paper is reviewed, the managing editor will notify you of the results. There are three possible outcomes of the review process:

- **Accept without modifications** - This is the Holy Grail and a rare occurrence. It means that the reviewers think that your paper is ready to be published without any changes. A very low percentage of all submitted papers are accepted as-is without further changes. If you get a letter like this, do a little dance. You have written a great paper!

- **Reject** - In this case, based on the comments of the peer reviewers, the editor has decided that your paper is unsuitable for publication in that particular journal, and that no amount of modification will make it possible for you to publish that paper in that journal. Don't fight this decision; it is usually final and irrevocable.

The best thing to do is to take the reviewers' comments to heart, discuss the comments with your coauthors, determine whether the paper can be revised, and then consider another journal. Most decent journals have a rejection rate of about 50%, so this is a more common occurrence than you might think from the number of papers that are published every year. Like in the music business, there is a lot or rejection in the research business.

- **Accept with revisions** - This occurs in about 45% of all papers submitted for publication in peer-reviewed journals. This result means that the reviewers opined that the paper would be acceptable for publication after certain comments are addressed and changes made. The editor-in-chief then reviews the reviewers' comments, and if she/he agrees that the comments were fair, those comments are then sent to you for a response. This gives you a chance to improve your paper, sometimes dramatically. Oftentimes there are valuable insights in the reviewers' comments. Revisions could be:

  ➢ **Major** – the reviewers suggest that the paper needs significant changes. For example, the reviewers suggest that you add new data or that you significantly change your conclusions. In this case, fulfilling the reviewers' suggestions will require a significant amount of work.

  ➢ **Minor** - revisions that can be accomplished by rewriting text and/or presenting the same data in different ways.

Responding to the reviewers' critiques

If you receive a review that includes a request for revisions and you want to publish in that journal, you must respond to <u>all</u> the comments of the reviewers, even if there are some comments you don't agree with.

After receiving your review, you must respond as soon as possible (sometimes within 48 hours) with your revised manuscript <u>and</u> a letter detailing the changes that you've made in response to reviewer comments. You must respond and/or resubmit by the deadline provided in your letter or request an extension of the deadline if there are major revisions.

If you delay in sending your resubmission, your revised manuscript may not be considered a revision. Instead, the editor may choose to treat it as a new submission, starting the review process all over again. You don't want this to happen! So make it a priority to respond quickly to the review.

To respond, write a letter addressed to the editor-in-chief acknowledging receipt of the reviewers' comments. Express gratitude to the editor for his or her reply, and to the reviewers for the time and effort they devoted to reviewing your manuscript. Then, in the letter or in a separate attachment mentioned in the letter, you must address each of the reviewers' comments one-by-one, either noting the change you made in response to the reviewer's comment, or giving a thorough explanation as to why you did not make the change.

Please keep in mind that you do not need to make every single change suggested by the reviewers, but your explanations for not making specified changes should be clear, logical, and respectful.

I recommend that you cut and paste each of the reviewers' comments and reply beneath each one. Even if this is not required, it is a good idea to organize your response in this way. (Some journals actually provide a template for exactly this purpose). Note that when a response to a reviewer's comment requires a change in the manuscript text, the page number where the change will appear should also be included in the response. If multiple reviewers make the same suggestion, it is okay to refer to your previous response, as shown in the following example of a response to reviewers' comments.

Note that some editors may send the paper back for re-review to the same reviewers (or to different reviewers) after you have entered your revisions. The editor may ask the reviewers to determine if your responses sufficiently address their concerns. In that case, reviewers may send additional comments and recommendations during a second round of revisions.

Even if you make all or most of the changes that the reviewers suggested, there is no guarantee that the paper will be published in that journal. The editor-in-chief still has the final say as to whether the changes were sufficient to make the paper publishable in their journal.

Example of response letter to reviewer comments

Dear Dr. Editor-in-Chief:

RE: Article #JSH12345

Thank you for your reply concerning our submission titled "Asthma Rates in the Latino Population." We appreciate the reviewers' comments and found them helpful and insightful. We have incorporated the majority of their suggestions, which we believe strengthen our manuscript significantly. The individual reviewer comments and our responses are detailed below. Our responses are in italics.

Reviewer 1, Comment 1: Asthma rates vary by ethnicity in the United States with Mexican Americans having the lowest rates of asthma, and Puerto Ricans experiencing the highest rates of the condition. However, the authors combined data from both ethnic categories. I think that both groups should be examined separately in sub-analyses.

Response: We agree with the reviewer's comment and have included additional analyses that compare asthma prevalence among Mexican-American and Puerto Rican children in our sample. These results can be found on pages 9 and 10. These results are also now presented in Table 3.

Reviewer 1, Comment 2: In Table 2: The authors indicated that they included non-respondents in the denominators. Have the authors tried deleting the non-respondents? How would that affect the results?

Response: We thank the reviewer for this suggestion. The results did not change when non-respondents were deleted, so the original analysis was kept in the article.

Reviewer 2, Comment 1: In the analysis, the non-responders were included. I think these data points should be removed from the analysis, and only those who responded to all questions be included.

Response: We appreciate the reviewer's suggestion. As discussed in our response to the first reviewer's comment #2, we redid the analyses excluding the non-respondents and found no difference in the results. Thus, the original analysis was kept in the article.

The publishing process

 Okay. So, you have written a clear paper that contributes new scientific information to the literature. You have received and applied the constructive suggestions of the reviewers, made the necessary changes to the manuscript, and intelligently responded to any criticisms that didn't apply. You wrote a clear and respectful letter to the editor detailing all the changes, and you are now waiting for a final decision.

If the editor believes that you have sufficiently responded to the reviewers' comments, he or she will send you a letter of acceptance. At this point, you can consider your paper as "in press," and you can cite it in other papers and include it in your curriculum vitae. You can only cite the paper as in press if you have a final decision letter stating that it has been accepted.

To cite the paper, write the citation including the author names, the title of the paper, the journal name and the words "in press" in place of the journal volume, date and page numbers. Once it is published, you will add the journal details at the end of the citation.

The next communication that you will receive will be from the managing editor, who coordinates the typesetting of your paper. Depending on the journal, a copyeditor may also contact you as he/she reviews the paper for grammar, format, proper citations and punctuation; they may also request minor writing changes.

Before the paper can appear in print, galley proofs will be sent to you. These are mock-ups of what the paper will look like when in print, usually in PDF format. You must check and double-check these page proofs. Go over them with a fine-tooth comb! This is your last chance to catch any mistakes, misspelled words, and grammatical errors. This is also your opportunity to provide typesetting instructions to the printers.

This is not the time, however, to make any major edits to the paper. If you do, it will be considered a new paper and it may be returned to you. Also be sure to return the proofs by the requested date. A delay in returning the proofs can mean a delay in being published.

When checking the proofs, you can mark-up a printed copy using the most common proofreaders' marks to avoid any confusion as to the desired changes. A list of proofreaders' marks can be easily found online. These are standard symbols used to indicate things like "add a space" or "insert paragraph". Just be sure to communicate with the journal if you are unclear about how you should note changes and approve the proofs. You should also attach a list of page numbers that have changes so they will not be overlooked.

Another simple option, since there are usually only a few minor changes needed at this point, is to provide a clear list of the changes using an "Is: Should Be: format". At one time publishers wanted authors to sign and return the marked-up page proofs. Now an email approving the proofs with noted changes is usually acceptable.

If an important piece of information has come to light since you submitted the paper, some journals allow for authors to include an *Addendum in Proof* that is then added at the end of the paper without disrupting the typesetting. This must be a truly important piece of new information that will significantly enhance the paper and can be given in a very brief statement.

Depending on the backlog of submitted papers that the journal receives per publication period, there could be a lag between the acceptance of your paper and the time your paper actually appears in the publication. This lag period can range from weeks to several months depending on the publication rate of the journal, the number of papers that they publish per issue and other factors. Journals include the date of acceptance for each article, so you can determine the average lag time by comparing it to the publication date. This will give you an idea of when you can expect to see your paper published.

Journals also publish the date of receipt. The date of receipt and the date of acceptance are especially important in highly competitive areas of research where it might be important to know who first reported an important finding. Recognition as the "first to discover" is then determined by these dates.

With the galley proofs, the journal will send you an order form for requesting reprints. These are professionally done, publication-quality reprints of the paper. Fewer and fewer authors request these reprints now since most readers will be able to access the paper online. Also, desk printers have improved so much in availability and quality, and journal reprints can be quite expensive.

However, as a first-time author, you may want official reprints to share with colleagues, attach to your curriculum vitae, and of course, send home to Mom. She will be proud of you! And you should be proud of yourself too! You are now an author in the peer-reviewed literature.

So, you published a research paper. Now what?!

First of all, congratulations! This is a MAJOR achievement. Publishing a research paper is a big score! A home run! A goal! A touch down! A gold medal.

Really, CONGRATULATIONS! This is a great victory. Celebrate it.

But your work is not yet over.

Remember how we talked about the importance of the journals' impact factors? Well, there has been increasing importance being given to the author's level impact factor. One such metric is called the h–index. The h-index is intended to measure the productivity of a scientist by calculating the citation impact of his/her publications. Although its use is not yet widespread, I have started to see it more and more included in candidates' curricula. I predict that this trend will continue to increase and will become a measure that could help or hurt researchers' careers in academia.

For instance, the h-index could be used to set standards for promotions to higher faculty levels. It could also be used for appointment and promotion committees to decide between comparable curriculum vitae, as some positions are very competitive. The h-index could offer a quantitative indicator of a candidate's past productivity and future promise.

The h-index is a measure of both the number of papers a researcher has published and the number of citations per publication. It is calculated at the intersection between the *h* number of papers that an author has published, which have been cited at least *h* number of times. You can see this graphically in figure 1.

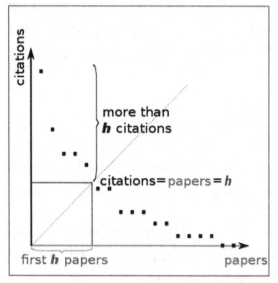

Figure 1: Calculating the h-index for authors

Remember, you want your paper to be seen by those who would be most impacted or interested in your data. The h-index is just a quantifiable measure of how your papers are being used and have impacted research in any way.

However, there are some issues of concern regarding the h-index. One is that it does not measure whether the paper is being cited because other people are building on those studies or because it is being refuted in many different papers and that is why it is being cited. Another issue is that there are several databases that can automatically calculate an authors' h-index. Among them are Web of Knowledge, Scopus, Research Gate and Google Scholar. Each database may calculate a different h-index because they may have access to a different number of papers or journals to make the calculation.

Another major issue is that an author's h-index can vary widely between disciplines. For example, an h-index in the 2-3 range might be good enough for tenure in sociology, but you would need it to be at least a 12 to make it to tenure in physics, according to JE Hirsch's 2007 paper in *Proceedings of the National Academy of Sciences*. It is not yet clear whether appointment and promotion committees are taking these differences into consideration when evaluating faculty productivity.

If you stop working on your paper once it is published, you will miss out on a lot of opportunities to capitalize on your achievement. Notice that the older a paper gets, the less likely that it will be cited. After publication, your paper lives in a small little space in the cyber universe. Without your help promoting it and making it known that your discovery is now available for everyone to see, it will languish there without receiving much attention. Here are some ways in which you can increase the chances that your paper will be seen, read, understood, appreciated and hopefully, cited.

(Note that many science journals imposed an embargo on the papers they publish. This means that after your paper has been accepted, you cannot publicize the paper until it is actually published in the journal. The period between the acceptance and actual publication is the embargo. Before you make your paper widely known in the press, check with your journal to see whether they impose an embargo period.)

Send out an email blast

At this stage in your career, I am sure that you have accumulated a long list of contacts who work in similar fields as you. Colleagues who may be interested in the results of your latest study include people such as former mentors, collaborators, students and interns who have worked with you, contacts that you have met at conferences, familiar people who work in similar areas of research, and to people whose work you have cited in your list of references in the paper.

Since all of these are professional contacts, you can communicate with them in fairly technical language. To send an email communication to this group, you can just cut and paste the abstract of your paper to your email message, attach a PDF of the paper to the email, and use the title of the paper as your subject heading. You may want to preface the email message by saying something like this:

"I thought that you would be interested in our latest paper that has just been published in the latest issue of Journal of Mad Science (vol 123: 12-19). In it, we report that gene x regulates G-protein signaling for hematopoiesis and its role during the inflammatory response. Below we include the abstract. A reprint of the full paper is attached. Thank you, Me."

The purpose of this email blast should be to inform your colleagues about your discovery, to elicit discussion and feedback, to start a conversation about topics of interest, and to increase the chances that your paper might be cited by these colleagues. Although these colleagues ideally should be able to find your paper during their literature search when they are writing their own articles, it can be helpful to send it directly to those who may be interested and could benefit from the information.

In addition, I like to send copies of my research papers to research participants in population-based studies, if it is appropriate and permissible under institutional review board (IRB) guidelines. Check with your IRB for guidelines regarding this if you are interested in distributing your research paper among study participants. At least consider sending a copy to leaders of community-based organizations who may have facilitated your study or might in some way be interested in the results of the research that was conducted in their community. Do not underestimate their role or their interest in the research outcomes.

Social media

You might consider blogging on your own website and posting your research papers as part of your blog, or writing a summary of your paper intended for a broader audience. You can summarize your paper in a blog-style format and post it on Facebook, Twitter, LinkedIn, etc.

It's important to keep in mind, however, that the publishing journal now owns the copyright to your paper. For that reason, it is not always clear whether you are free to distribute your paper that broadly unless it has been published in an open access journal. In that case, anyone who clicks on the link should be able to access it without having to have a subscription. In this case, simply write a short summary of your main findings for a lay audience and include a link to the paper. You can easily check if your paper is freely available by finding the citation in PubMed. After the PMID number, it will say "Free Article" or "Free PMC Article" in red letters.

ResearchGate is becoming increasingly popular as the social networking site for scientists and researchers. By becoming a member of the website, you can share research papers (both published and unpublished), post questions, make announcements, follow other researchers, have them follow you, receive and give endorsements for different skills, share data, and work collaboratively on shared documents.

The network grows by sending out domestic emails to coauthors of researchers who join. It also sends out automatic emails every time one of your papers is cited, or if one of your coauthors or a person you follow publishes a new paper. ResearchGate also issues an author impact factor called an RG score that has been criticized for its validity, because the algorithm used to create it is not published.

That said, I do use ResearchGate, especially to keep up with my students' publications. I find it helpful to receive a notification whenever a student publishes a paper. However, joining yet another social media network may not be to everyone's liking.

Press and traditional media

Popular media is increasingly covering scientific studies and breakthroughs. Most TV newscasts now have segments on science- or health-related news during which they publicize the results of recent research. Many newspapers have whole sections on science and/or medicine either embedded into the daily news or as separate special sections. There are also news magazines and specialized science magazines that report on science and medicine for the general public.

Many research scientists are reluctant to reach the general population through the media. Perhaps they considered their work too esoteric to be of interest to the public. Others may feel that journalists may misinterpret their results, and fear it may lead to a media outlet misquoting them or otherwise misrepresenting them or their findings. Yet others may think that it is not worth their time to talk to reporters when approached, much less to reach out to the media unsolicited.

All three viewpoints are understandable to a certain degree. My argument is that if your research can benefit the world, then the world needs to know about it.

There are several ways for you to be cited in the media. Sometimes journalists who are in a science or medicine beat may reach out to specific scientists to request interviews. Alternatively, journalists may contact the press office of the academic institution where research is being conducted and request a referral to scientists that may be knowledgeable about their topic of their investigation.

In either case you are obliged to contact the press or media office at your institution to let them know about the media request. Different institutions have different policies for responding to media. Check in your faculty handbook or call your media officers for guidance in this regard.

Another way in which your research can end up in the press is by issuing a press release. The press release is that communication directed at members of the news media to let them know about something newsworthy that they may or may not decide to publish. A press release can be issued by the journal where your paper is published or by your institution. Or, you may decide to issue your own press release. Press releases can be sent to all types of media including radio, TV, online magazines and newspapers.

Typically, a press release should be just one to three pages long, and it should capture the importance and newsworthiness of the report. It should be written in a style that very much mirrors the way that newspaper articles are written. In fact, sometimes newspaper articles are copies (almost *verbatim*) of press releases.

If you decide to issue a press release of your paper, check with your institution's press office about contacts for distribution and any rules that your institution may have as to how researchers may approach the press. Your press release should have the following sections:

- **Headline** – it should be attention grabbing, and state very succinctly what the news is about.

- **Deadline** – this should state the release date of the news, the city where the news originated from, and if there is a news embargo before which you are requesting the news not to be released.

- **Introduction** – this section would give the basic important information.

- **Body** – this should be an expanded explanation of what was stated in the introduction such as any supporting data and elaborating details. It is important that the body also includes quotable text that includes a citation to the person or persons to whom the quote can be attributed.

- **Boilerplate** – this is the "about" section where you state who the person providing the news is or the company they represent.

- **Close** – this is just a symbol to indicate that this is the end of the press release (no other pages are to be added), and it can be indicated by adding this "###" or the statement: "end of release"

- **Media contact information** – this should be either the actual scientist responsible for the research and/or the institution's press office. It should be given either at the top or bottom of the press release.

Following is an example of a Press Release issued to announce the publication of my study: Claudio L, Tulton L, Doucette J, Landrigan PJ: Socioeconomic factors and asthma hospitalization rates in New York City. Journal of Asthma 36: 343-350, 1999.

Although a little bit old, I am showing it to you here because this press release was responsible for catapulting the information all the way to the New York Times.

Embargoed For Release   Contact: Greta Newsman (212) 555-5555
July 27, 1999   Catherine Mann (212) 555-5555

ASTHMA HOSPITALIZATION RATES IN POOR NYC NEIGHBORHOODS
UP TO 5 TIMES HIGHER THAN THE CITY AVERAGE

— Harlem, Bushwick, Mott Haven, Hunts Point Worst Hit;
New Study Pinpoints Asthma Hospitalization by Zip Code, Income —

July 27, 1999, New York. An analysis of New York State hospital discharge data by zip code, income level and minority status in New York City was recently published. Hospitalization rates for asthma in the 34 hardest hit neighborhoods are 21 times higher than in the least affected communities, and up to five times above the citywide average. The study was conducted by researchers at the Center for Children's Health and the Environment at Mount Sinai School of Medicine, a project funded by The Pew Charitable Trusts, and published in the June/July issue of the Journal of Asthma.

The ten zip code areas identified as having the highest rates of asthma hospitalizations were 10029 (East Harlem/south, Manhattan), 11237 (Bushwick, Brooklyn), 10035 (East Harlem/center, Manhattan), 10454 (Mott Haven, Bronx), 10030 (Central Harlem, Manhattan), 10474 (Hunts Point, Bronx), 11221 (Bushwick/Bedford-Stuyvesant, Brooklyn), 10455 (The Hub/Longwood, Bronx), 10456 (Morrisania, Bronx), and 10451 (Melrose, Bronx). The lowest rates were found in lower Manhattan and some Queens neighborhoods. The study also found that high hospitalization rates correlated with low median household incomes. In addition, the percentage of children under the age of 18 was higher in zip code areas with high asthma hospitalization rates, as was the percentage of minorities.

"Medical experts and community leaders have long been concerned that air pollution may be related to asthma" said Dr. Luz Claudio, the study's lead author. "These findings provide strong evidence to suggest that socioeconomic factors can influence access to preventive care, poor housing conditions and exposure to air pollutants, all of which can contribute to the development and progression of asthma."

(continued on following page)

Asthma is a complex disease with multiple causes. Attacks are triggered by a series of factors and typically occur when genetically predisposed individuals encounter environmental triggers. Many low-income, inner-city homes have several such triggers, including indoor and outdoor air pollution.

"It is distressing to see so many children suffering from asthma in our neighborhoods," says Leon Tulton, a college intern who lives in the South Bronx who is coauthor of the study. "I wanted to contribute to finding out why this is happening." Mr. Tulton helped conduct the study as part of an internship program for minority students and community residents at Mount Sinai.

Other community residents and members of neighborhood organizations have conducted their own community-based research projects to help determine the causes of these high levels of asthma. We Stay / Nos Quedamos and the West Harlem Environmental Action Group have been conducting a survey of the fumes from diesel-fueled truck traffic through their residential streets. They believe that the diesel fumes may contribute to high asthma rates in their neighborhoods.

Asthma is a chronic disease of the lungs and airways characterized by periodic attacks in which the airways become partially blocked. Attacks result in difficulty breathing, coughing and wheezing. There are nearly 15 million people with asthma nationwide; a third of them are children. Asthma accounts for 10 million lost school days annually—the leading cause of school absenteeism attributed to chronic conditions. Asthma leads to 2.2 million pediatrician visits per year and one in six of all pediatric emergency visits in the U.S. The annual cost of treating asthma in children is estimated at $3.2 billion.

To help address the growing problem of pediatric diseases such as childhood asthma that may be triggered by environmental exposure, Mount Sinai School of Medicine has established The Center for Children's Health and the Environment, the nation's first academic research and policy organization exploring the links between childhood illness and exposure to toxic pollutants. The Center is a project funded by The Pew Charitable Trusts.

# # #

Points to remember from Chapter 11

- The manuscript should be submitted through the journal's online portal. A cover letter should be included and directed to the editor-in-chief.

- When you submit a paper for consideration in a journal, three things could happen: it could be rejected, it could be accepted with minor or no changes recommended, or it can be accepted with major changes recommended.

- There are a number of people who will be involved in the publication of your paper. These are:

  - The editor-in-chief oversees all publications in the journal and has the final say as to whether your paper is published in that journal.

  - The editorial board is composed of experts in scientific disciplines related to the topic of the journal. They may also provide specific subspecialty editorial input to the journal.

  - The managing editor is the person who first screens your paper upon submission and works to administer the review and publication process.

  - Reviewers are experts in the same field that you are—your peers. They are unpaid volunteers who provide their comments and opinion on your paper to ensure that it meets good standards. They make their recommendation to the editor-in-chief on the merits of your paper, determine whether it's worthy of publication in the journal, and make suggestions and recommendations for improving the paper.

- You should respond to every comment provided by the reviewers by either accepting their recommendations and making the changes in the paper, or explaining why you have not made those changes.

- The revised paper should be accompanied by a letter that details your response to each of the reviewers' comments. The tone of this letter should always be respectful, even when you might disagree with the comments.

- Consider different ways of promoting your paper in order to increase its visibility and impact.

Exercise 11: Research paper writing plan

RESEARCH PAPER WRITING PLAN:

Step	My deadline	Date completed
Gather data and decide what to include in the paper		
Consult with collaborators about data interpretation		
Create tables and graphs for paper		
Outline the paper		
Organize the literature and materials using the outline		
Draft title		
Gather instructions for authors of possible journals		
Write methods section		
Write results section		
Consult collaborators on draft of methods and results		
Write introduction section		
Consult with collaborators		
Write discussion		
Send draft to collaborators for review. Give them a deadline for response		
Incorporate collaborator comments and/or discuss further.		
Decide on a journal.		
Write abstract and title page		
Final edit of paper based on journal guidelines, including formatting of reference section		
Paper submission		
Critiques received and sent to all coauthors		
Write letter response to the editor and reviewers		
Edit paper according to critique		
Resubmit		
Promote the publication of your paper		

You may go to www.drluzclaudio.com and download the forms for this exercise, which you will be able to customize to fill in.

Chapter 12: Tips, Hacks and Tools

"Procrastination is the art of keeping up with yesterday."

– Don Marquis, American poet and author

The previous chapters of this book have given you step-by-step instructions about how to write your research paper. If you have been writing at the same time as reading the book and doing the exercises, you are probably close to having a paper ready for submission to a peer-reviewed journal. As you continue to write and publish your research, you will learn some shortcuts, tricks and tools of the trade that will help you along the way. Much of the knowledge of how to write a research paper will come from just doing it. Years of experience will make it easier and easier for you.

In this chapter, I will give you some knowledge that I've gained through 25 years of writing research papers. Much of this knowledge comes from trial and error.

By no means is this a complete list of tips, hacks and tools. I am constantly learning new ways to increase my writing productivity. I update my readers with any new helpful hints in my blog and in the course Write Science Now (www.WriteScienceNow.com). To keep up to date with writing tips, hacks, and tools, or to get more details about the ones given here, make sure to visit my website (www.drluzclaudio.com) or become a member of our course community. If you are interested in enrolling in the online course, please send an email through the contact form on my website and you will be added to the waiting list.

Tips for increasing writing productivity

By far, the number one hurdle that most of us have to surmount is the overwhelming feeling of not having time to write. Writing can feel like another task to be added to the long list of to-dos. There doesn't seem to be any time in the day as it is. Adding yet another thing to do can certainly seem daunting. However, because of the portents of writing and publishing our research papers, we must make this an integral part of our daily habits, if not at least our weekly habits.

Here are some tips to increase your writing productivity. Please use, change or adapt any that may help you get those papers published now.

- **Start with a mind map**: Sometimes it helps to start your paper by drawing a diagram of your paper or papers—a mind map. Start your mind map by drawing the central most important concept for your paper. Then draw branches emanating from that central concept that divide further from the most general to the most specific sub-branches, until the diagram looks like a spider or a sunburst. Basically, a mind map is a flow diagram with the branches going in many different directions.

  The main utility of mind mapping is for you to visualize how your results may relate to the central concept and to each other. Some of the utilities of a mind map are:

  - Drawing the mind map by hand helps me rapidly visualize all of the work I have done on a particular project, and makes it easy to see how different outcomes may be related to each other.

  - Mind mapping gives me an idea of how many papers I may need to write from one particular investigation or research focus. Sometimes this happens when it is obvious that different branches emanating from the central research concept go in singular directions and do not connect. This may be an indication that another central concept may have emanated from those results, which should be reported in a separate paper.

- **Use the Pomodoro technique**: As we discussed earlier, you want to motivate yourself to beat the clock by setting up mini deadlines that help you to focus solely on writing for a well-defined period of time. This time-management technique was developed by Francesco Cirillo in 1980 and has been adapted to many different types of productivity issues. It entails using a timer to set 25-minute intervals of intense focused work on a particular task. (Cirillo used a kitchen timer shaped like a tomato, hence the name *pomodoro* meaning *tomato* in Italian). When the timer goes off, take a short 3-5 minute break, then go back to the task for another 25 minutes. After 4 of these 25-minute intervals, take a longer break. According to this author, this is the optimal ratio of intense work and rest. More information about the Pomodoro technique can be found here: http://baomee.info/pdf/technique/1.pdf

  Some people find that the ticking noise and alarm of the timer add to the sense of urgency intrinsic in the technique, which makes them more focused and intent on completing the task. Others, like me, find the ticking noise too stressful. I use a modified version of the technique by playing instrumental music on my earphones while I write. I set the music on a timer that goes off with a pleasant bell rather than an alarm. This helps me get into a writing rhythm and propels me forward. For some people, the type of music may also have a beneficial effect on their writing motivation. As long as the music does not have words, I find it helpful.

Yet another modification to this technique is using the word count as your unit of measure instead of time. This can be helpful because it is possible that you can set up a timer or music for using the Pomodoro technique and yet end up writing very little. Therefore, it may be necessary for you to have an additional measure of productivity besides the time spent in front of the computer. Although word count may not be the best measure of productivity, perhaps it will give you a very easy way to assess how much work you have done.

- **Temptation bundling**: This is a concept developed by Katherine Milkman, PhD, of the Wharton School of the University of Pennsylvania to study behavioral economics. However the concept can be applied to many different activities in which willpower and determination are needed to complete a task that may not be immediately rewarding. In one of the examples that she studied, people who had decided to exercise more were given very "addictive" audio books that they could only access at the gym while they were working out. The audio books motivated the study participants to exercise at the gym more often as compared to participants who did not have that incentive.

  Similarly, you could create a "temptation bundle" to motivate your writing by combining something that you like with the task of writing. For example, I listen to certain classical music that I like only when I am writing for research papers and grant proposals.

  Another example may be that you only allow yourself to sit in a place that you like such as a balcony while you are working on your writing. Think about things that you can allow yourself to have only while you are writing. The music is very effective for me, but you may have other ideas of ways in which you can trick yourself to achieve your writing goals.

- **Writing accountability partner**: Just like dieting or exercising, writing can also be enhanced by sharing the experience with somebody else was also going through a similar situation. Is there somebody else on your research team (at or near your level) who has to write papers as well? A person like that can be a great accountability partner for you and you for them. If you are a postdoctoral fellow, it should be easy to find other fellows in your institution who might want to partner with you to motivate each other into writing papers. You can also use your accountability partner to receive feedback on your writing, check each other's work, and keep each other encouraged, especially when other people may not understand your need to write.

- **Use dictation software**: Some people find it difficult to sit for long hours in front of a computer typing away. For some, just the physicality of it is strenuous. For others it can just be difficult to think as a writer. However, you may find it very easy to talk about your work. In fact, sometimes your writing is improved by dictation because in may sound more fluid, coherent, and clear. You can also dictate while walking around your office. You can even dictate into your phone, and then transfer that dictation into your document. Even though I can type quite fast, I often use dictation to help with the speed and quality of my writing. Of course, with dictation you are prone to make more errors, but you would have to edit your document anyway. Try dictation and see if it might increase your productivity.

- **Read more**: It has been said that nothing makes a better writer than a good reader. This is very true for research writing. Although I do recommend that you read the papers that you would use for citation while you're writing, making a habit of reading research articles in your field is a must. So, not only do you need to read papers for keeping up with the literature and finding out what's going on in your area of research, but you also need to read research papers for the purpose of learning how to write well.

  As you read other people's research papers, notice the language used, the phrases that occur repeatedly, and the terms most often used to refer to certain concepts. Notice how the paragraphs are structured, how the data is presented in the figures and tables, and how it is compared to the existing literature in the discussion section. I bet that you have not often noticed these things in research papers. Rather, you have been reading to extract information for your own research. Noticing these aspects of the research literature will help you immensely in your own scientific writing.

- **Remember that time is time**: I used to think that I was only able to write at the end of the day after everybody had left the lab, when I was most likely to have a long chunk of time to dedicate to writing. So, I used to get home at 11 o'clock at night every night.

  By using the outline to identify sections of a paper that I can write in shorter periods of time, I am now able to find shorter periods of time during the day when I can still be productive in my writing. Another helpful change that I have made in my schedule is that I try to prioritize writing by doing it first thing in the morning before other distractions and priorities set in. I have created a habit of making myself a cup of tea when I first come in in the morning and opening up the writing file to work on the paper or grant proposal that is closest to being finished, or that has the most urgent due date. Even if I only have 30 minutes before my first interruption of the day, writing in the morning has trained me to know that writing is a priority.

- **Don't fight writer's block**: Writer's block can happen at any time. Whether you are just starting to write a paper or even if you are in the middle of writing one, writer's block can attack. Suddenly no words come to mind, and the flow of ideas just stops.

When you find yourself in this situation, don't fight it. And most importantly, don't give into that feeling. Instead, do something peripheral. Even if it feels small, it still advances your paper. Use the time that you have allocated to writing to work on another activity related to the paper, even if it is not writing text.

For example, you can re-read papers stored in your outline file, or call a collaborator to discuss a result, or you can work on formatting your figures and tables. Whatever you decide to do, don't quit doing work related to your paper. Doing any of these things will likely get you unstuck so you can proceed with the writing later on.

- **Serve as a reviewer**: Because of the volume of research papers that is submitted to peer-reviewed journals, editors are always looking for additional reviewers. If you have already been published in a certain topic, make sure to mark your availability to review in the journal's website. If you have not published before, ask your mentor to give you papers to review the next time he or she gets asked by a journal.

Serving as a reviewer will teach you how to critique a paper, notice mistakes that authors make, and help you to experience the publication process from the other side. Being able to critically review a paper should be part of every scientist's research training.

- **Beware of junk journals**: During the early years of my career, journals were funded by paid subscribers, professional societies, advertisers. The only revenue that was solicited from authors was related to post-production charges (after the paper had been accepted for publication). These included "page charges", (for printing color illustrations, for instance) or reprint charges, for obtaining journal-quality copies of the manuscript.

The advent of open-access journals (in which the author pays a fee to the publisher) combined with the pressure to publish has resulted in the rise of predatory publishers. The original idea behind open access was that the journals would make their publications available to everyone, without the need to have a paid subscription. Legitimate open access journals, engage the peer review and editorial process and charge authors after the paper has been accepted for publication. Unfortunately, this open access format has fueled the rise of predatory publishers that exploit research authors by charging a publication fee without providing a thorough peer-review or editorial service. These fake journals will publish anything as long as someone pays for it. Imagine! Researchers have submitted manuscripts written by randomly generated text, and the papers have been "accepted" for publication in these types of journals.

As you become a published researcher, you will start receiving email invitations to submit articles to journals that you have never heard of, but that may have titles that are similar to journals that you already know. You may also receive invitations to join the editorial board of "new" journals. Do not fall for these scams! Most of these are made-up journals that are not peer reviewed and are not listed in reputable repositories such as Pubmed. Their sole purpose is to get you to submit your manuscript and pay for publication in an "open access" format.

I receive solicitations from these bogus journals <u>every day</u>! Some have become so adept at trying to fool me that they copy the format and approximate the name of journals on which I have previously published. Some indications that the email that you have received is from a predatory publisher are:

➤ You are receiving unsolicited email from a journal in which you have never published. Unless you are a member of the editorial board, the only email that you should be receiving from a journal are:

- Correspondence regarding a paper that you have submitted.

- The table of contents of upcoming issues of the journal.

- Requests for you to review a paper submitted to the journal.

➤ The email lists fake members of the editorial board or lists scientists without their permission. To test this, you may do a search of the names listed as members of the editorial board to see if they exist, if they are affiliated with a reputable academic institution and if they list membership on this editorial board in their curriculum vitae.

➤ The journal is not listed in PubMed or any other reputable repository of scholarly articles, and the journal does not have an impact factor listed on Web of Knowledge.

➤ Your manuscript is reviewed quickly, and you receive minimal comments, if any. Soon after, you receive invoicing for publication of your paper. Let's hope that you don't get this far, but if you do end up submitting a paper to one of these journals, DO NOT send any money until you are completely sure that it is a legitimate journal.

The website **_Scholarly Open Access_** publishes a list of predatory publishers and predatory journals every year (some publishers may have dozens of journal titles under one publisher). Go to https://scholarlyoa.com to check their lists if you are unsure about the authenticity of an invitation that you have received. Or go to the website just for fun. You will be amazed at some of the outrageous bogus journals currently circulating and the endless attempts to get money from authors. Please beware!

- **Believe**: It may sound cliché, but it is because it is true. Believe that you can do this. See yourself being published and anticipate the thrill of it. Being intent on achieving this goal is probably the most important tip, hack or tool that I or any other mentor can give you in this journey.

Exercise 12a: My ideal research workweek

Think about what your ideal workweek would be like. First, enter the tasks that you are required to do that occur at a specific date/time. Then, add important required tasks that you must do, but that do not have a set time for doing them, including writing. Add some fun time to your schedule too, to keep you motivated.

Example: Ideal Workweek of a Postdoctoral Research Fellow in his Second Year

Time	Mon	Tue	Wed	Thu	Fri
8 am		Jog at the park	Write paper	Dance class	
9 am	Write paper	Write paper	Teaching assistant office hour	Write paper	Write paper
10 am			Lab experiments		
11 am	Lab meeting			Meet with biostatistician	Meet with colleague
12 pm	Walk and lunch	Department seminar series	Postdoctoral work-in-progress lunch	Division Seminar Series	Grand rounds series
1 pm	Lab experiments	Lunch with friend		Data analysis time in super computer	Lab experiments
2 pm		Lab experiments	Attend course lecture and study group		
3 pm				Lab experiments	
4 pm			Meeting with principal investigator		Study time
5 pm	Attend course lecture	Study time	Prepare data for analysis	Study time	Attend course lecture

Exercise 12b: My ideal research workweek

Think about what your ideal workweek would be like. First, enter the tasks that you are required to do that occur at a specific date/time. Then, add important required tasks that you must do, but that do not have a set time for doing them, including writing. Add some fun time to your schedule too to keep you motivated.

Time	Mon	Tue	Wed	Thu	Fri
8 am					
9 am					
10 am					
11 am					
12 pm					
1 pm					
2 pm					
3 pm					
4 pm					
5 pm					

You may go to www.drluzclaudio.com and download the forms for the following exercises, which you will be able to customize to fill in.

Inspiration from testimonials

Motivation, consistency, focus, drive, commitment, and determination; these are some of the things that you need to be an accomplished published scientist. It's not just about having great data. You must believe that you can do this, make it a priority, and push through to complete the task.

This book is dedicated to my students, because it has been through them that I have learned everything that I have included in this book. Every idea and recommendation that I have included here, I have tried and tested first on the students, trainees, postdoctoral fellows, visiting scholars and junior faculty that have worked with me over the many years that I've had as a faculty member.

Some of them have provided their testimonials here to help motivate and inspire you to achieve the same success. I hope these stories inspire you as much as they have inspired me through the process of writing my first book.

I met Dr. Claudio on 2012 as an Intern of Mount Sinai's Preventive Medicine Department. I never thought that working with Dr. Claudio could help my career and me as a person in so many ways. First, she helped me overcome the fear of writing in English. Second I had the opportunity to work in Puerto Rico's Pediatric Environmental Health Sub-Unit (PEHSU) as fellow of Mount Sinai School of Medicine.

In 2014 I had the opportunity to work again with Dr. Claudio, but this time from Murcia, Spain under the mentorship of Dr. Juan Antonio Ortega. There, I participated in several investigations; as a result, we published two more papers using the techniques in this book. These experiences awakened in me the desire to work to change the environmental reality of children, both in my country and around the world. In summary, Dr. Claudio has helped me grow a seed that already existed but needed nourishment. Changes in public policy are achieved through research published in scientific journals and who is better to teach us through her book how to do so than Dr. Claudio a person with so much expertise in the field.

Glory Ann Rivera Pagan, DrPh

I was excited when Dr. Claudio gave me the opportunity to work with her as part of a short-term internship program. I had just completed a master of public health degree in epidemiology. Research was not something new to me; I had previously published articles. Nevertheless, while working with her I soon found out that there was still much more for me to learn about how to craft a manuscript.

I loved working with data and had strong analytic skills, but performing data analyses was only one part of being a successful researcher. Once I finished my analyses, I needed to be able to tell a story with my results— and a pretty succinct story at that (about 3000-3500 words).

As a person who loves data I tended to think that all my results were interesting and I wanted to present them all. I learned some important lessons from Dr. Claudio as she reviewed drafts of the manuscript we were working on together. She taught me the importance of using the results section to describe key findings or trends rather than simply describing all the results found in the tables. I could give examples of specific findings from the data tables to support the key findings/trends, but I needed to use the results section to present what the data in the tables meant rather than simply presenting the data from the tables.

It has been many years since I finished that internship, but these lessons are still at the forefront of my mind and I am sharing this valuable information with others.

Sasha McGee, PhD, MPH

The summer after I graduated from my undergraduate studies I had the pleasure of participating in Dr. Claudio's training program. From this program, I not only gained a unique opportunity to work with international researchers, but also was introduced to Dr. Claudio herself, who became an important academic and professional mentor to me in the years to follow. Since my initiation into the international exchange program, Dr. Claudio pushed me to challenge myself to be the best researcher that I could be.

Through the program and her constant guidance, I was not only able to present my research at an international health conference in Switzerland but also to publish a research paper as first author in a prestigious journal. My initial collaboration with Dr. Claudio led me to taking an opportunity as a research assistant directly to her at the Preventive Medicine division of the Mount Sinai School of Medicine. Here, I was able to work with Dr. Claudio to study the effects of training programs on students' attainment in research and medicine careers. Dr. Claudio worked with me every step of the way to improve my critical thinking, analytical, and writing skills, and eventually to complete a manuscript submitted to academic journals on higher education.

My work with Dr. Claudio has opened many doors for me. After working with her, I went on to conduct an independent Fulbright research project in Brazil, as well as participate in several other public health research projects both abroad and in the U.S. Today, I am a doctoral student studying Mental Health at the Johns Hopkins Bloomberg School of Public Health and cannot be more grateful to Dr. Claudio for allowing me the opportunities and professional mentorship that have gotten me here today.

Noa Krawczyk, PhD Candidate

I had the pleasure of meeting Dr. Luz Claudio through my acceptance into the Mount Sinai International Exchange Program to Dublin, Ireland. Passionate and driven to pursue a medical career, my journey lacked guidance. Dr. Claudio pushed me to become a better version of myself. She believed in my potential to excel and saw within me what I, myself, had not seen at the time: my potential to succeed.

With the encouragement from a strong mentor, I became inspired. Most importantly, I learned to humbly and confidently believe in myself. I worked harder than I had ever worked and was able to publish my very research paper. Not only am I the first author, but also it was published in the journal *Nature*. I could not believe it! Now, my second piece of work is also in press!

Rarely in life do we run into people who believe in our potential to achieve more and genuinely mean it. Throughout my life, I have been told several times that I was not going to make it: that I was not good enough, not smart enough and that I did not have what it took to be successful. Instead of allowing me to believe this, Dr. Claudio pushed me to believe in myself.

Throughout my journey, Dr. Claudio has always extended her warm and caring nature towards me. She was (and still is) always willing to help in every possible way while never allowing me to sell myself short of any successes. She has high standards that she expects all of her students to reach and I appreciate that. I believe in the impact this book will have on those who read it because I have had the pleasure of getting to know the person who stands behind it, and am honored to not only call her my mentor, but also my friend.

Angela Nilda Flores

There are skills beneficial for a specific job, and then there are those skills that transcend time and profession. Doctor Luz Claudio has helped me develop one of the latter. Producing a paper of experimental results is as important as the scientific process itself. This is something I first understood as an intern in one of her training programs.

Less than a year ago, I was given the opportunity to travel to Murcia, Spain to conduct pediatric environmental research. Needless to say, working in a foreign country on scientific research was a mind-opening challenge and an enriching experience to my career as a public health scientist. However, I believe the most important lesson learned during my tenure in the program was how to draft and refine a scientific manuscript. Molding literature reviews and original data analysis into a manuscript that supports a rational scientific discussion and robust conclusions requires much skill and experience, both of which were provided by my program mentors.

Dr. Claudio's guidance during the past year has helped me take large strides towards achieving two ambitious goals that have shaped me into a more qualified public health scientist. Thanks to Dr. Claudio, I now have submitted a manuscript for publication in a peer-reviewed journal. She is also guiding me in the process of writing and submitting an abstract to a national public health conference.

I continue to apply manuscript writing skills on a daily basis at my current position as a field epidemiologist, where I oftentimes am in charge of writing up findings of epidemiological investigations. Being able to clearly and concisely report scientific results is a skill that very well complements and strengthens my prior data analysis and interpretation abilities, and one that I will likely use for the rest of my career.

Henry Andres Olano-Soler, MPH

I still remember when I was about to finish a master's in public health in epidemiology, but did not know how to utilize it. I felt lost because the public health area is very broad. It was then that I stumbled upon an opportunity to apply to a summer research program led by Dr. Luz Claudio. I needed a lot of mentoring at the time, but the program did more for me than just mentoring. It provided me with the skills needed to succeed as a professional in the health field.

Before leaving for my summer research opportunity, I was able to learn about various aspects of research such as writing a research paper, data analysis, and how to work with our mentors. Throughout my clinical research experience in the field of pediatric environmental health, I learned that research requires a team effort. In addition, I was able to coordinate various aspects of research studies, shadow physicians, and engage with research participants. After putting so many hours of hard work, I had the privilege of coauthoring a research paper which was published in a peer-reviewed journal that same year.

I am very thankful for being accepted into one of Dr. Claudio's programs. First of all, it reassured me that I have a competitive edge to apply for a position that only a small percentage of applicants get an acceptance. Ever since the research paper was published, employers and educational programs are amazed by the fact that I have a publication on my resume. It has allowed me to stand out from the crowd.

Now that I am a first year medical student, I can say that I am more than just a future physician. I know that I will also be able to contribute to the literature in clinical research which will help many communities. Overall, I am confident that this book will be a very essential resource for anyone writing a research paper.

Jorge E. Gutierrez, MPH, MD Candidate

I participated in Dr. Claudio's training program in the summer of 2013, after yearning for an experience to research, learn, and grow. Dr. Claudio's role as a mentor and teacher began on my first day of orientation in New York City, and continues to this day. I was immediately impressed with her knowledge of not only writing and publishing research, but also of how to proceed through research projects in order to make a substantive contribution to science.

After working on my research, Dr. Claudio's mentorship and lessons about writing and publishing research papers were directly applicable. After a lot of writing, editing, and refining my research paper, our project was accepted at the 5th International Congress on Arsenic in the Environment. In Buenos Aires, Argentina, I gave a talk about our research to an international community of scientists. Without Dr. Claudio, I would have never had the abilities nor the confidence to share my findings, in both written and oral form.

This experience led to being awarded a Fulbright research grant to conduct research in Mexico. Studying adolescent mental health, I felt prepared and ready to go, having been trained on conducting and communicating research. Just last month, my Fulbright research was published. As I wrote this paper, I constantly employed the writing skill sets and lessons that Dr. Claudio gave me. Her wealth of knowledge and mentorship have helped me more than I can express, and I know she will continue to help students grow and thrive as both scientists and people.

Aubrey Herrera, MPH

Index

CPSIA information can be obtained
at www.ICGtesting.com
Printed in the USA
LVOW05s0129310517

536394LV00004B/12/P